CW00347033

# early bird 1

Teacher's Book

# early bird 1

**Teacher's Book**

**David Vale**

The right of the
University of Cambridge
to print and sell
all manner of books
was granted by
Henry VIII in 1534.
The University has printed
and published continuously
since 1584.

CAMBRIDGE UNIVERSITY PRESS

Cambridge
New York   Port Chester   Melbourne   Sydney

Published by the Press Syndicate of the University of Cambridge
The Pitt Building, Trumpington Street, Cambridge CB2 1RP
40 West 20th Street, New York, NY 10011, USA
10 Stamford Road, Oakleigh, Melbourne 3166, Australia

© Earlybird Publishing 1990

First published 1990

Printed in Great Britain by Bell & Bain Ltd, Glasgow

ISBN 0 521 40976 4 Teacher's Book 1
ISBN 0 521 40977 2 Student's Book 1
ISBN 0 521 40978 0 Class Cassette 1
ISBN 0 521 40979 9 Home Cassette 1

## Author's acknowledgements

The author would like to thank the many people who have helped
and inspired the development of *early bird*.

Special thanks to:
Ana Vale for a constant stream of creative input. Brian Johnson,
for visual inspiration. Ken Jackson, for a truly gifted view of
primary school education. Oliver Norman, for putting *early bird*
into the classroom. Simon Gieve, for helping at the start. Stephen
Mullaney, for many brilliant ideas in primary education.

And to the staff and children of Richmond Hill Primary School,
Cumbria, England. The director, teaching staff and children at the
English School, Sevilla, Spain (especially Alison, Beverley, Noel,
Patricia and Rosalia).

The directors and teachers at Language Resources in Kobe,
Japan.

And to my editor and children – for much more than inspiration.

WD

# Contents

# Map of *early bird 1*

| | The Children's Experience of Language Input across the Curriculum | | | Language Output from the Children in an Activity-Based Context | |
|---|---|---|---|---|---|
| | Activities and topics | Teacher's questions, instructions, and comments about: | Physical Response Activities | Vocabulary | Expressions and structures |
| 1 | measuring and personal measurements | measuring distance, height, weight; recording results of measuring | stand up<br>reach up<br>put up<br>put down<br>stretch<br>higher<br>wider<br>relax<br>sit down | numbers 0–10<br>*basic colours*<br>eye<br>hair<br>foot<br>hand<br>centimetre | me<br>her<br>him<br>yes/no<br><br>I'm, he's, she's |
| 2 | displaying photos and cartoon pictures | family and family photos; neatness and display skills | stand over there<br>stand back<br>smile<br>say | *family members*<br>*pets*<br>numbers 11–20<br>my<br>your<br>his<br>her | taller than . . .<br>smaller than . . .<br>older than . . .<br>younger than . . .<br><br>This is . . .<br>Who's this . . . ?<br>Is this . . . ?<br>I'm . . .<br>He's/She's . . .<br>Maria's (possessive s) |
| 3 | beetles<br>beetle games;<br>number games | making a beetle; playing beetle; numbers and simple arithmetic | draw<br>throw<br>cut<br>glue<br>pick<br>say | *parts of the body*<br>numbers 21–31<br>long<br>big<br>little<br>round<br>dice<br>a/the | my turn<br>your turn<br>his turn<br>her turn<br><br>It has (got) . . . |

Map

| | The Children's Experience of Language Input across the Curriculum | | | Language Output from the Children in an Activity-Based Context | |
|---|---|---|---|---|---|
| | Activities and topics | Teacher's questions, instructions, and comments about: | Physical Response Activities | Vocabulary | Expressions and structures |
| 4 | Picture Dictionary | sorting and classifying words; displaying cut-outs | hold up<br>point to<br>cut out<br>glue in<br>count<br>put under | ketchup<br>hamburger<br>french fries<br>hot dog<br>pizza<br>*colours*<br>*food*<br>*numbers* | I do/don't<br>here/there<br><br>Maria's, Toni's . . .<br>(possessive s)<br><br>Who has . . . ?<br>Who is . . . ? |
| 5 | making a Snapdragon | cutting and folding; spelling; playing *Snapdragon* | colour<br>pick<br>fold | *colours*<br>first<br>next<br>last<br>another<br>mine<br>yours<br>his/hers | finished<br>like this<br>How do you<br>   spell . . . ?<br>heads or tails<br><br>I like/don't like |
| 6 | cartoon story | identifying pictures; organising picture information; storytelling; acting and role play of the story | pick up<br>squeeze<br>open<br>bite | Review | bald head<br>Hi!<br>lots and lots<br><br>. . . bites, puts, opens, goes (present simple) |
| 7 | dot picture; facts about elephants | numbers; drawing and colouring; parts of the body; information about elephants | stand up<br>come here<br>pick up<br>put down<br>say<br>join | teeth<br>trunk<br>ears<br>right<br>left<br>numbers –<br>   100–1000<br>its/their | please<br>thank you<br>plus/minus<br><br>eats, weighs, lives, equals (present simple) |
| 8 | Picture Dictionary | sorting and classifying words; using a dictionary | hop<br>measure | art and craft<br>family<br>tape measure<br>scissors<br>eraser<br>pencil<br>glue<br>numbers<br>   100–1000 | in tens<br>How tall . . . ?<br>Can I have . . . ?<br>Here you are.<br><br>You're going<br>   to . . .<br>(future) |

| | The Children's Experience of Language Input across the Curriculum | | | Language Output from the Children in an Activity-Based Context | |
| --- | --- | --- | --- | --- | --- |
| | Activities and topics | Teacher's questions, instructions, and comments about: | Physical Response Activities | Vocabulary | Expressions and structures |
| 9 | making a *favourites crest* | likes and dislikes; favourites; using charts to record information | hold<br>open<br>lick<br>swallow | favourite<br>toy/game<br>*foods*<br>*drinks* | I do/don't<br>my favourite . . .<br>is . . .<br>me too<br><br>How many . . . ?<br>How much . . . ?<br>Do- questions<br><br>I like/don't like . . . |
| 10 | face shapes; making a mask | observing face shapes; sorting shapes; making a mask | draw | shape<br>round<br>square<br>triangle<br>rectangle<br>egg<br>heart<br>big<br>medium sized<br>small<br>mask<br>parts of the face<br>ugly/pretty | I don't have . . .<br>Can I borrow . . . ?<br><br>Do/does questions<br>he/she/it has a . . .<br>I/you have a . . . |
| 11 | Picture Dictionary | sorting and classifying words; using a dictionary | Review | Review of foods, drinks, colours and games | Do you want<br>   a . . . or a . . . ?<br>(four) of us<br>How many . . . ?<br>some/any<br><br>Review of present simple and future (going to) |
| 12 | *ring a ring of roses*; circle shapes | observing, sorting and classifying circle shapes; organising picture information | this way<br>   round<br>the other way<br>   round<br>throw<br>watch<br>catch | circle<br>ring<br>roses<br>pocket<br>long<br>thin<br>twisty<br>balloon | both hands<br>one hand<br>. . . plus . . . equals<br>wide/long<br><br>holding,<br>walking,<br>running . . . etc.<br>(present continuous) |

# Introduction to *early bird 1*

## Principles

### *early bird* is activity-based

*early bird* is a truly activity-based language course. It teaches primary school activities through the medium of English, encouraging children to accept English as a communication tool, and to use it as part of an overall learning experience.

*early bird 1* has two themes: *ourselves* and *shapes*. Within these themes children listen, understand and take part in a series of cross-curricular activities in English. The children develop their English gradually and systematically in an activity-based context. Through the activities, the children are introduced to a wide range of everyday English. At the same time, the teacher is able to focus attention on the specific language items that arise in each unit of the course. The children are guided along a learning pathway which starts with input and experience, and ends in speaking.

### How *early bird* works

The activities have been carefully chosen to reflect children's interests, while at the same time covering a wide range of accessible language points. *early bird 1* contains twelve Units. Each Unit is taught in three clearly defined phases:

- **A Preparation phase** involving a series of *physical response*[1] games using the key language needed for the Main Activity phase.

- **A Main Activity phase** in which the children complete a practical topic. This hands-on experience of language creates a natural text for guided practice in the Follow Up phase.

- **A Follow Up phase** in which the teacher uses the confidence and experience gained by the children in the previous two phases of the Unit to encourage them to speak. At this stage the teacher can focus on specific language points.

Although the nature of *early bird* allows both children and teachers to work at their own pace, the course is designed so that each phase can be completed within one lesson. Each Unit, therefore, usually takes three lessons to complete. However, the interest of the children in a particular topic or activity is always to be encouraged and some Units (e.g. Unit 1) will need more class time.

[1] See notes on PR Activities, page 6.

## *early bird* and the learner

*early bird* treats learners as individuals. As they learn English, the children build up their own personal *early bird* book by recording their practical classroom experiences and incorporating information about their personal interests, opinions and abilities. Activities extend beyond the classroom into everyday life. The children share with their parents (and even teach them) what has been achieved in class.

*early bird* never forces children to speak before they are ready. Throughout the course the children are introduced to language through a variety of physical and practical activities. The children become relaxed and confident with English before speaking it. This removal of fear of failure is a key factor. Children are encouraged to speak – and they will speak well – when they are ready to speak.

## The advantages of *early bird*

- The children study activities which have practical educational value. These activities parallel the type of study which is common in mainstream primary education all over the world.

- The children are motivated and interested in what they are studying. *early bird* puts *their* needs first.

- The children are introduced to a wide range of natural English from Lesson 1 of the course. This language is meaningful and understandable because the activities are meaningful and understandable.

- The children are taught in English. There is no need to translate into their mother tongue.

- The children are not tied to learning English in an artificially pre-determined sequence of grammatical structures or functions. They are learning about their world – in English.

- Children can be taught in mixed ability groups. Children with more English will speak more about the activity they are doing – and help lower level classmates at the same time.

- *early bird* gives the teacher the total content for each lesson. It is a complete course.

- The learning focuses on the individual. The children build up their own personal journals within their English course. These are exciting and accurate records of what they have achieved, and are theirs to keep.

# Components

*early bird 1* is the first of a series of five *early bird* books and materials which are now being successfully taught in language schools all over the world. There are four components:

Student's Book 1
Teacher's Book 1
Class Cassette 1
Home Cassette 1

## Student's Book 1

The Student's Book is designed for the children to complete: they record their own practical classroom experiences, incorporating information about their interests, opinions and ideas onto page layouts that encourage student-centred learning.

– *your early bird course* (page 1) is a picture index for *early bird 1*.

– *bits and pieces* is a space on the inside front cover where the children can attach an envelope. This makes a practical pocket for small take-home material.

– The *star chart* is a straightforward, easy-to-see grading system which is printed on the inside back cover of the book. The children are awarded colour stars, Unit by Unit, according to achievement or performance. The children are encouraged to take on the responsibility for this assessment themselves, choosing a colour with which to grade their own or each other's work, rather than relying on the teacher for evaluation.

The content of the Student's Book can be sub-divided as follows:

### The Activity Pages
The left-hand pages in the first part of the book (pages 2–24) provide activities which have practical as well as linguistic educational value.

– The activities are cross-curricular. They include: *arts and crafts, mathematics, music, picture dictionary work, picture puzzles, social studies, storytelling.*

– Because of the nature of specific activities, several of the Activity Pages need to be cut up and are therefore printed in the *Activity Cut-Outs* section at the back of the book. The children will eventually re-assemble these cut-outs, or store them in a *cut-outs envelope* on the appropriate page in the book.

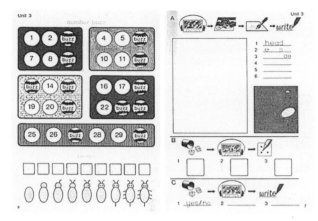

Activity Page          Workpage

### The Dictionary Activity Pages
The Dictionary Activity Pages review and preview the key vocabulary from the course. They are introduced at regular intervals: Units 4, 8 and 11 in *early bird 1*.

– The vocabulary is presented in picture form, with the written words printed under each picture. The children sort and classify this vocabulary by *category,* for example: *colours, food and drink, games and toys, numbers.* Once classified, the children glue the items onto the appropriate page, and under the appropriate category, in their *early bird* books.

– The Dictionary Activity Pages need to be cut up, and are therefore printed in the *Activity Cut-Outs* section at the back of *early bird 1* (pages 27, 35 and 39).

– The children also file these vocabulary items in their own, independent Picture Dictionary. The Dictionary Activity Pages are therefore printed in duplicate. The children use the items from pages 29, 37 and 41 for their independent Picture Dictionary. The printed words are omitted from the duplicates.

### The *Activity Cut-Outs* Section
This section, printed at the back of the book, contains all the Activity Pages that need to be cut up by the children.

### The Workpages
The right-hand pages in the first part of the book (pages 3–25) review and reinforce activities that have been done in class.

– In the early units, instructions are given in picture code form. As the course progresses, the picture codes are gradually replaced by the written form.

– The parents are involved. By checking the responses their children record on the Workpages, parents are able to share the progress that their children are making in class. Parents should be encouraged to sign each Workpage to indicate they are taking an interest in their children's English course.

## Teacher's Book 1

The Teacher's Book is intended as a guide for the experienced teacher, and as a professional resource for those working with children for the first time. The Teacher's Book:

– introduces the basic principles of the course and outlines the teaching approach and procedures for *early bird 1*;

– contains a course map which indicates the vocabulary and potential language points for each activity topic in the course;

– clearly explains the aims of each step in a Lesson. Guidance is also given so that, if necessary, teachers can adapt specific activities to their individual classroom situation;

– provides an *overview* page at the beginning of each Unit which summarises each step in the Lessons and lists the course components to be used;

– gives detailed practical Lesson plans for every step of the course.

## Class Cassette 1

This Cassette focuses on the key language points for each Unit. It includes the sorts of questions children would expect to be asked about the results of their practical activities. The Class Cassette:

– communicates directly with the children by asking them questions, and giving them instructions. It is a practical classroom tool for the teacher;

– is recorded with young voices;

– contains recordings of the *Physical Response* scripts with special sound effects which convey the *feeling* of the language;

– contains traditional songs, rhymes and chants which are recorded with young voices. The songs, rhymes and chants have been chosen and adapted to complement the main themes and topics in the course.

## Home Cassette 1

This Cassette contains extracts from Class Cassette 1 and provides the listening input for the Workpages. With your guidance, it can be used at home by the children and their parents.

Parents should be encouraged to play the Home Cassette and follow their children's responses so that they can share their children's progress through the course.

## The children's Picture Dictionary

The children make their own, independent Picture Dictionary, using the headings and items from *early bird* as a central core. For more detailed information on this Dictionary refer to pages 41–2.

# Using the course

## The cross-curricular approach

The cross-curricular activities in *early bird* are the main focal point for each Unit. In this way:

– Children are introduced to a very wide range of language through the activity-based content of the course. They gain an active understanding of everything the teacher says, but are not required to repeat it.

– Children are encouraged to speak about the Main Activity, and the results of their class work. This involves concentrating on specific language points.

– Children are encouraged to work on the language of the *Physical Response* (PR) Activity. In addition to providing a source of language input for the Main Activity in a Unit, each PR script therefore becomes a language text in its own right.

– There is constant re-cycling and review of language.

## The standard teaching framework

It is very important to establish a routine when teaching children. This removes the confusion and insecurity that children naturally feel in the first lessons of a course. Once children are familiar with what is expected of them, the day-to-day running of the course becomes much easier. Moreover, children can be encouraged to take over the teaching role in classroom routines such as taking the register, setting up the classroom layout, and giving instructions to begin or end an activity.

Although the activities within this routine vary greatly, the overall Lesson format remains fairly constant. Each Unit of the course is taught in the three phases mentioned earlier. Namely:

– **A Preparation phase** involving a series of *physical response* games with the key language needed for the Main Activity phase.

– **A Main Activity phase** in which the children complete a practical topic. This hands-on experience of language creates a natural text for guided practice in the Follow Up phase.

– **A Follow Up phase** in which the teacher uses the confidence and experience gained by the children in the previous two phases to encourage them to speak. At this stage the teacher can focus on specific language points.

The three phases of an *early bird* Unit are taught in various stages. These form a *standard teaching framework* which the teacher can use as a guide for presenting the content of each Unit. The table opposite shows the phases, typical stages and teaching sequence for an *early bird* Unit.

In addition, the teaching notes for each Lesson contain a *Preparing your Lesson* section. This tells the teacher if there are any materials (e.g.) flash cards, that may need to be prepared in advance.

## The stages of an *early bird* Lesson

### Warm Up

The purpose of the Warm Up stage is to create a focal point for the attention of the class at the beginning of a lesson. The children come to class from various previous activities and locations. A short Warm Up activity helps them to forget out of class distractions. It also establishes a positive attitude for the lesson ahead.

In *early bird*, Warm Up activities develop in the following way:

Lesson 1 – a fun, work together activity
Lesson 2 – develops from the Action Game in Lesson 1
Lesson 3 – develops from the Warm Up / Action Game in Lesson 2

The importance of starting every lesson with a Warm Up activity cannot be overstressed. These activities are not merely ice-breakers. The content of the Warm Up is an integral part of the overall learning content. The children are introduced to relevant language, and more importantly, encouraged to work together and help each other – an essential feature of learning with the *early bird* course.

### Presenting New Language

In *early bird*, new language content is determined by the topic or theme of the Unit. In Lesson 1 of a Unit the children are introduced to the English they will need for the Main Activity. In Lesson 2, the children are given further experience of this language within the Main Activity itself. Finally, in Lesson 3, they are encouraged to practise specific language points when, for example, they talk about the results of their practical tasks.

New vocabulary is introduced in a visual context with the use of picture flash cards or real items. *early bird* encourages children to become familiar with the flash cards (items) through physical activity. The children, for example, are asked to:

*Point to a flash card, pick it up and give it to a friend, copy it, draw it on a friend's back with a finger, stand near it, put their hands up if they're holding it, hide it, find it, turn it over, shout at it, say their names if they're holding it, mime it, race for it, touch it, play twister with it, take it home and give it to their parents, etc.*

## A Teaching Framework for *early bird* Units

| Lesson 1<br>Preparation Activities | Lesson 2<br>The Main Activity | Lesson 3<br>Follow Up Activities |
| --- | --- | --- |
| Warm Up: a group formation activity | Warm Up: a group formation activity using the PR script from Lesson 1 | Warm Up: a group formation activity using the PR script from Lesson 1 |
| Check Homework: feedback on the previous lesson; the children evaluate the previous Unit in pairs; check parent's signature and comments | Check Homework: feedback on the previous lesson; check what the children have brought in | Check Homework: feedback on the previous lesson: check the children have completed the homework task |
| Presenting New Language: input of key words for the Main Activity using a PR approach | Main Activity: chat to, encourage, praise the children informally while they work | Language Practice (1): focus on the language point derived from the Main Activity in the previous lesson |
| PR Activity: input of short text – language from this text relates to the Main Activity – use the Class Cassette | Tidy up: *tidy monitors* give the instructions | Language Practice (2): do the Workpage activities – use the Class Cassette |
| Review Activity | Review Activity – use the Class Cassette | Review Activity (e.g. song or chant from the Class Cassette) |
| Homework: ask the children to bring in necessary items for the next lesson | Homework: ask the children to complete their Activity Page for the Unit | Homework: ask the children to complete the Workpage activities – encourage parental involvement |
| Round Up: a group formation activity | Round Up: a group formation activity | Round Up: a group formation activity |

For a detailed example of the procedure for introducing new vocabulary, turn to pages 14–15, where the numbers 0–10 are presented.

The procedure should take between 15 and 20 minutes. The children are involved the whole time. The activity starts with the children taking responsibility for recognising one word only. By the time the activity ends, all the children will have had the chance to teach each other all the words.

## Action Games / PR Activities

The Action Games are based on a short sequence of instructions or descriptions. The content of this sequence has been specifically designed to relate directly to the language or theme of the Main Activity of the Unit. Action Games are essentially *Physical Response* (PR) Activities[2]. *early bird* has adapted PR Activities to suit the needs of the course.

The initial purpose of an Action Game is as a preliminary teaching tool. The children respond to a sequence of instructions, questions or descriptions without speaking. They gain confidence and active understanding of the language they need for the Main Activity without the stress of having to produce this language correctly at too early a stage. As the Unit progresses, the Action Game script is developed into a language teaching text in its own right. The children are encouraged to teach this text to their classmates, and finally to their parents.

The Action Games are recorded on the Class Cassette. Most of the recordings contain special sound effects which convey the *feeling* of the language.

The children use Action Games throughout the course. An Action Game is introduced in Lesson 1 of a Unit. In Lesson 2, the Action Game is reviewed and used as the Warm Up activity. In Lesson 3, the Action Game is reviewed again as the Warm Up activity. At this stage children are encouraged to focus on the language and produce it themselves. For detailed examples of the procedures involved refer to pages 15, 18 and 20 in Unit 1.

Class size and classroom layout are important factors for PR Activities. If the desks and chairs are movable, make the first step of the Action Game a series of moving furniture instructions. Encourage the children to give these instructions. In a more traditional classroom setting, and with large classes, create a demonstration space in the classroom. Ask groups to demonstrate and get the remainder of the class to comment on performance. Adapt the Action Game to suit your classroom environment.

---

[2] Teachers who wish further background information on PR, or TPR (Total Physical Response) should refer to Dr James Asher, *Learning Another Language Through Actions: The Complete Teacher's Guide Book* (Los Gatos, California: Sky Oaks Productions, 1977).

## The Main Activity

The fundamental goal of *early bird* is that the children take away from the classroom something of practical educational value every lesson. You teach in English. The children learn in English. Your role is that of a primary school teacher, or parent, or good friend – as well as that of a language teacher.

The way you teach the Main Activities in *early bird* will depend on factors such as the age (developmental) and ability of your class, the number of children in the class, classroom facilities, your own teaching skills and experience. Each Lesson plan in this Teacher's Book makes extensive practical suggestions. However, there is no substitute for hands-on experience. The following, therefore, is intended as a general guide.

i.   If this is the first time you have used the course, you must prepare in advance. It is advisable to try out all the practical activities to check on details and potential problems.

ii.  Make sure the children have everything they need for the activity. Make this a homework assignment if necessary. Always bring in lots of spares in case any children leave important items at home.

iii. Teach the practical skills that the children need before they do the activity. Encourage suggestions, ideas and opinions from the children. If they can't explain it in English, let them show you. In Unit 1, for example, teach the children how to measure height accurately with a tape measure. Ask them to show you good and bad ways of measuring.

iv.  Encourage the children to guess or estimate results before they do an activity, then let them compare their findings with their guesses. Use lots of gestures as you speak to help put across the meaning of your questions, explanations and instructions. For example in Unit 1:
Teacher: *How tall are you, Barbara?*
Student: *One, four, two centimetres.*
T: *How far can you stretch? Guess.*
S: *One, two, five centimetres.*
T: *Tomiko and Hiroshi. Can you check, please. How far can Barbara stretch?*
S: *One, four, zero centimetres . . . etc.*

v.   During an activity keep important equipment within easy reach of all the children. After the activity make tidying up an essential part of the lesson. Choose a tidy monitor for each group.

vi.  Use an *everything must stop* signal, two loud claps, for example. Always insist everything stops when you use this signal.

vii. In the early part of the course, teach the children the English they will need for the usual classroom conversations. For example:
S: *Can I have a pencil, please?*
*I don't have an eraser.*
*Can you pass me the glue?*
*I can't see.*
*I've finished.*
*I don't understand.*
*How do you say . . . in English?*
*Can I go to the toilet, please? . . . etc.*

viii. Double check that the children have everything they need: *pencils*, *glue*, *scissors*, and so on before you ask them to start an activity.

ix. Ask the children to complete unfinished gluing and colouring for the homework assignment. They can put any loose pieces of paper in the *bits and pieces* envelope.

x. Establish a routine so that the children know, for example, where to find materials and how to organise the classroom layout for activities. The activities in *early bird* are extremely varied and will challenge and stimulate your class.

xi. Encourage friendship in the class with activities that involve personal contact and support. A relaxed and friendly atmosphere not only lowers barriers to learning caused by stress and tension, it also discourages unwanted cliques.

xii. Establish a class behaviour code. Bear in mind that motivation, interest and involvement are without doubt the best forms of discipline.

xiii. Allow quiet times. Learning takes place during drawing, cutting and gluing. Chatting to the children in English while they are working is part of teaching.

xiv. Experiment with classroom layout. Organise the desks and tables to allow the children, and yourself, the space to move and work freely. Treat any re-organisation as a language teaching opportunity. It is well worth spending a few minutes moving tables and chairs, since this can make all the difference to the success of an activity. If the desks and chairs are difficult to rearrange, create a demonstration area in one corner of the room.

xv. Display the children's work. Use classroom walls, a washing line across the room, a corner of the classroom. If it isn't practical to use wall space, saving the children's work in a giant Class Book is an excellent alternative.

## Language Practice

The activities in *early bird* generate a natural range of language both from the teacher and the children. In terms of a new learner of English, most of the language will be in the form of input from the teacher, and through the activities. In *early bird 1*, the language output from the children is carefully monitored. It is developed systematically as follows:

– non-verbal response;

– key word/phrase response;

– guided speaking;

– spontaneous speaking.

In the early Units, at beginner level, the children give short, appropriate, true answers about the activity they've just done. For example:

T: *How tall are you, Ana?*
S: *One, three, nine.*
T: *How about you, Barbara?*
S: *One, four, two . . . etc.*

In addition, *early bird* allows the teacher to focus on specific language points. The completed Main Activity acts as the language text. For a detailed example turn to page 39.

The Class Cassette is an important teaching aid to language work. The exercises on this Cassette communicate directly with the children, for example, asking the children questions about the results of the activity they have just done. In Unit 1, for example, the activity is measuring and recording personal information:

*Tapescript*
*Part 3. Listen and give true answers.*
1. How old are you?
2. How tall are you?
3. How much do you weigh?
4. How long is your foot?

*Part 4. Listen and give true answers.*
1. How high can you reach?
2. How far can you stretch?
3. How high can you jump?
4. How far can you hop?

It is also important to add your own questions and instructions in language work[3]. For example:

T: *Stand in a line. Tallest at the back, shortest at the front. Who's the tallest? Put your hand up. Who's the smallest? Put your hand up. Maria, how tall are you?*
S: *One, four, two centimetres.*

---

[3] Note: after completing the practical task, the children will be able to understand the general meaning of a wide range of relevant questions, and will be able to give you short, appropriate responses. However, they are *not* expected to produce or repeat your questions and instructions at this stage in the course.

The classroom layout is very important for language work. Consider in advance if you want the desks organised for pairwork (e.g. *children turning their chairs to face each other*), group work (e.g. *four children sitting around two desks*), or for the class working as one large group (e.g. *the desks against the wall and the children sitting in front of the desks, in a semi-circle*).

## Review

Review activities are an integral part of the *early bird* programme. Past Units are reviewed on a systematic basis. This is usually accomplished by reviewing a Unit which is three Units prior to the one being studied. (The children will review aspects of Unit 1, for example, while they are studying Unit 4; and consolidate language from Unit 2 while they are studying Unit 5, etc.)

The children invest a considerable amount of time building up their *early bird* books and Picture Dictionaries which, as personal records of work done, are the ideal texts for review purposes. Furthermore, when the children look back on their work, it will give them a great sense of achievement to be able to use, and to talk about, their own English textbook.

In addition to review, language is re-cycled and developed throughout the course. A cyclic approach to learning is essential in teaching children. The activity content of later Units has been adapted to ensure that this need is extensively catered for.

Finally, although the Lesson plans suggest the timing and content of the review activities, it is appreciated that the class teacher is in the best position to judge exactly when, what, and how much review should be done.

## Giving and Checking Homework

You give and check homework assignments every lesson. The tasks you assign are easy to complete, even for the busiest child. Typically, in each Unit, the homework assignments are as follows:

Lesson 1: You ask the children to bring in items for the next lesson.

Lesson 2: The children complete, or review their completed Activity Page.

Lesson 3: The children complete the Workpage exercises.

Homework is important because it acts as a bridge between lessons. Even if the task is minimal, it serves to remind the child of the work being done in class. Equally important is the fact that it can involve the parents. By checking the responses their children record on the Workpages, parents are able to share the progress their children are making in class. Informed and happy parents are an invaluable source of support for children and teachers alike.

In addition, in order to motivate the children to do the homework, it is essential to carry out at least a quick visual check that every child has in fact done so. Similarly, encouraging even minor aspects of a child's work rather than criticising work which has been done, will serve to boost the confidence of children who have tried their best.

Once the children have completed the Unit, they colour in the appropriate *star* in the *star chart.* The aim of this chart is to encourage children to evaluate their work. It is not a competitive evaluation. The class first evaluates your completed Unit in your book. The children then work in pairs, deciding the colour (for example: yellow = excellent; blue = good) their partners deserve.

## Round Up

This is a short, fun way to end each lesson. The aim is to bring the class together at the end of a lesson. In the same way that the Warm Up focuses the children's energy when they come into the class, it is equally important to focus their attention at the end of the lesson. In this way, the children leave the room with a sense of group identity.

The language content of the Round Up is related to the language used in the Lesson – or a previous Unit. The Round Up is therefore extremely valid and useful in terms of review. For example:

T: *Everyone sit up straight. Who's wearing something green? Ken and Toshi and David. Good. Now listen carefully. The first three children to put their hands up with the right answer can go. Who's wearing something . . . blue? Good. Ana, Margherita and Terri, you can go . . .*

# Notes from the author

A teacher using an activity-based course for the first time needs support and guidance. The approach is different. Many of the techniques and attitudes seem to conflict with traditional EFL methodology. On the other hand, teachers with experience of teaching children will realise that traditional EFL methodology alone does not work with children. *early bird* recognises that there is much of value within EFL methodology, but that the needs of the children must be put first. It is not within the scope of this book to enter into a discussion on learning theory. However, the following represents a summary of my experience concerning the teaching of children.

## Priorities

The priority for the teacher is to establish a working relationship with the children, and to encourage them to do the same with their classmates. Your role is that of teacher, parent, friend, motivator and organiser.

The skills you need for these roles have more to do with understanding children's development, children's needs, children's interests, the children themselves – than with EFL methodology. *early bird* encourages you to focus on areas such as relationships, classroom organisation, motivation, and allows children to achieve results at their own pace and according to their own abilities.

Young learners have specific learning needs. It is not sufficient to provide children, whether native or non-native speakers, with a programme of study which merely focuses on language, or indeed on any other isolated skill. Instead, it is necessary to offer a whole learning situation in which language development is an integral part of the learning taking place, and not the only end product. Moreover, it is impossible to know what children in any given language lesson can or will learn. What is known is that children learn best when they are involved. They learn best when they have the opportunity to experience and experiment for themselves, by *doing*. This means providing a range of child-centred activities.

Language activities for the sake of teaching language alone have little place in the children's classroom. For example, it is nonsense to ask the children: *Is there a book on the table? Is there a lamp on the table?* where the purpose of these questions is merely to teach *there is*. Children simply do not learn language one structure or six new words at a time. They learn language whole as part of a whole learning experience. It is the responsibility of teachers to provide this whole learning experience.

## Putting the children's needs first

There is a lot of pressure on the teacher to produce immediate, tangible results. Children need to be heard to speak English by proud parents. Administrators need concrete evidence of progress. As a result teachers tend to feel guilty if specific new structures and new words are not *learnt* every lesson. This is potentially a very harmful state of affairs. Moreover, if teachers insist on this type of achievement from children, they will inevitably encourage failure. Young children have no defence against this sense of failure. Children who have tried their best and failed to produce the result the teacher wants, will lose confidence and interest. They will feel, quite wrongly, that English is too difficult for them – and stop trying.

Children must be allowed to learn at their own pace. Language learning targets should not be forced upon them. Although it is widely recognised that children need a *silent period* during which they are introduced to language through a variety of practical and intellectual experiences, educators seem strangely reluctant to acknowledge that this fact also applies to the language classroom. Children will gain in confidence and motivation by studying English in an activity-based environment. They should be encouraged to work out for themselves what they want to say. They should be allowed to make mistakes without the fear of failure. In this way, you are laying the foundations for a successful language learner. Have no doubt, with *early bird*, children will speak in your classroom – and speak well – when they are ready to speak.

## Errors and correction

The long term aim of teaching English is for the students to speak English confidently, correctly and fluently. However, it is not reasonable or desirable to have this expectation at the beginning of a language programme. If you consider that an eight-year-old child may have ten or more years of language study ahead, then there is indeed much time available.

Therefore, in the early stages of a language course for children, it is important to establish priorities for the child as learner. These include:

- building confidence;

- encouraging ownership of language, children should experience English

- teaching children to communicate with whatever language they have at their disposal (mime, gestures, key words, drawings, etc.);

- teaching children to treat language as a tool for communication, not as an end product;

- showing children that English is fun;

- establishing a trusting relationship between teacher and children, and encouraging them to do the same with their classmates;

- giving children an experience of a wide range of language in a non-threatening environment.

In addition, repeated correction of errors at the beginning of a language course fosters the following negative aspects:

- Children lose confidence from the fear of making mistakes.

- Children only say what they know they can say.

- Children become dependent on the teacher for correction.

- The need for language accuracy interferes with the need to communicate.

On the other hand, there are certainly times when children do want to know how to say something correctly, in which case:

- Avoid correcting a child in front of classmates.

- Don't ask a child to repeat after you. It is much better to give a correct language example to a group of children, and let them teach each other.

- Accept good tries rather than aiming for perfection.

Experience has shown that errors made in the early learning days do not become so ingrained that the children themselves cannot be guided to recognise them, but this will only take place when they have enough experience of the language to make such correction meaningful and productive.

### The importance of group support

Speaking a foreign language requires the learner to take risks. To make mistakes in front of twelve or so others is a daunting experience for an eight-year-old child. Until children feel comfortable and secure in your class, they will learn very little. This sense of security takes time to develop. *early bird* has incorporated many activities which encourage group support, fun and friendship. Furthermore, to make the most effective use of class time these activities have been adapted to fit in with the theme or language of the particular Unit that is being studied.

### Using their bodies

Children need to have the opportunity to use their hands and their bodies to express and experience language. In an everyday context in an English-speaking country, children are quite naturally exposed to a variety of physical and intellectual experiences of language. In the foreign learning situation where children may have as little as one hour per week of English classes, it is vital that you include physical activities where the focus is on the physical response, and not on speaking.

The importance of providing physical learning opportunities cannot be overstressed. For children, this type of input is a crucial step in the learning pathway. With respect to activity-based study, and *early bird* in particular, many of the Preparation activities incorporate physical response. This provides a foundation of active understanding of the English needed in a Unit. When children do the Main Activity at the centre of the Unit, this language is given a practical context. The results of the activity – whether a chart, a badge, a beetle, or a collection of bottles – form a language text, created by the children themselves.

### The age of the learner

*early bird 1* can be used successfully with children from the age of six. The activity content of *early bird* has been chosen from activities which are re-cycled throughout the primary school years. Taking Unit 1 as an example, six-year-olds will need guidance in order to be able to use a tape measure whereas ten-year-olds should be able to estimate measurements in advance, and measure extremely accurately with a variety of measuring tools. However, the topic of measuring is relevant to both age groups. The language that is generated from the activity is also relevant to both age groups. The role of the teacher, therefore, is to make sure that the activity content is exploited to suit the developmental age of the children in the class.

### Organisation for Activities

Classroom organisation is a key issue in the teaching of children. For the practical activities in *early bird*, it is important that attention be given to classroom layout for group work, and to the assignment of *roles* to the children within their groups.

As stated earlier in this Introduction (Main Activity, section xiv) it is well worth spending a few minutes moving tables and chairs, since this can make all the difference to the success of an activity. Similarly, for ease of classroom management, the following roles can be assigned to children in each of the groups, before starting the activity:

- *tidy monitor* – responsible for making sure that everything is neat and tidy in the group at the end of the activity.

- *noise controller* – responsible for making sure that the noise level in the group is kept low.

- *organiser* – responsible for collecting and distributing equipment and materials to the children in the group.

- *English teacher* – responsible for making sure that whenever feasible, English is spoken in the group. The English teacher is also responsible for attracting your attention if there are any language questions.

For classroom management purposes, it is useful to make simple badges or name tags for each of these roles, and for the children who are assigned these roles to wear the appropriate badge. In addition, it is worthwhile bringing together the children who have a specific responsibility and to give them additional tuition, so that they may pass this information on to their groups. For example:

T: *All the 'English teachers', hands up. Come here please. I want to check you know these words in English . . . etc. . . . Now go back to your groups and help the others.*

## Equipment for *early bird* Lessons

All the activities in *early bird* are designed for use in the language classroom. No expensive equipment is required. However, it is necessary to have enough sets of scissors, glue (sticks), coloured crayons, and so on for children to use when they have forgotten to bring their own.

## The pace of a Lesson

In reality, pace is a matter of experience and intuition. However, the temptation is often to work too fast through the material, rather than to exploit the experience of the children. When children have successfully mastered an activity, it is often more useful to build on this success (e.g. encouraging more able students to share their success and knowledge with weaker classmates) than to move on to the next Unit. Similarly, once children have gained confidence in understanding a *Physical Response* (Action Game) text or description, it is worth spending time on challenging them to produce a correct spoken version.

The teaching notes suggest many changes of activity within one Lesson. This means that, in the Preparation phase, for example, the children will be introduced to language and content through a variety of short activities. Some involve movement, others are more passive. Since the attention span of young learners can be extremely short, varying the approach within a teaching sequence is very important.

The overall pace for the course very much depends on the teacher and the class. I have recommended around three Lessons per Unit. However, since one of the strong features of the course is that it is not tied to a linear sequence of structures, teachers should leave out that which they feel is too easy, too difficult, or not relevant to their particular classes.

Finally, as the author of the course, I sincerely believe that if you enjoy teaching children, *early bird* is a course that will give you the opportunity to teach them well.

# Information for the parents

Please copy (translate if necessary) the following information, and give it to the parents at the beginning of the *early bird* course.

Dear Parents,

I would like to tell you about the *early bird* English course.

*early bird* is more than just a language course. It gives children the opportunity to use English as part of an overall learning experience. This is a new and very different approach to the teaching of English.

Children study a whole range of practical and enjoyable primary school activities in English – in much the same way as they would at an elementary school in, for example, America, Australia or Britain.

*early bird* is not a course which forces children to speak before they are ready. In the early stages they listen, understand and do everything in an English-speaking environment, so that speaking follows naturally and spontaneously when children are ready to speak.

Furthermore, *early bird* involves you in the learning experience. Your children will bring home activities and teach you what they have been doing in class. It is important that you show an interest in your children's progress, and share their *early bird* activities.

*early bird* teaches children to use English as a communication tool. As a result, we sincerely believe that they will learn English well.

David Vale
Author, *early bird*

# Unit 1   Measuring

## INTRODUCTION

This Unit asks the children to measure themselves and record their measurements on the Activity Page (Student's Book page 2). The aims of this Unit are as follows:

– arousing interest in English;

– giving confidence;

– creating a supportive atmosphere in the classroom;

– socialisation: getting to know each other;

– enjoying learning English.

Through the practical activities in Unit 1, the children will:

– learn how to measure more accurately;

– record measurements;

– use *numbers 0–10*, and *colours of eyes, clothes and hair*;

– gain an active recognition of a wide range of question forms in English.

Table 1 (below) summarises the content of the Unit. Table 2 gives an outline of the key teaching steps.

Table 1

| The Children's Experience of Language Input across the Curriculum | | | Language Output from the Children in an Activity-Based Context | |
| --- | --- | --- | --- | --- |
| **Activities and topics** | **Teacher's questions, instructions, and comments about:** | **Physical Response Activities** | **Vocabulary** | **Expressions and structures** |
| measuring and personal measurements | measuring distance, height, weight; recording results of measuring | stand up<br>reach up<br>put up<br>put down<br>stretch<br>higher<br>wider<br>relax<br>sit down | numbers 0–10<br>*basic colours*<br>eye<br>hair<br>foot<br>hand<br>centimetre | me<br>her<br>him<br>yes/no<br>I'm, he's, she's |

Table 2

| Lesson 1 Preparation Activities | Lesson 2 Main Activity: Measuring (1) | Lesson 3 Main Activity: Measuring (2) | Lesson 4 Follow Up Activities |
|---|---|---|---|
| Warm Up: play *Chinese whispers* with names | Warm Up: Action Game: use Class Cassette Unit 1, Part 2 (follow Procedure 1) | Warm up: Action Game: use Class Cassette Unit 1, Part 2 (follow Procedure 2) | Warm Up: Action Game: use Unit 1, Part 2 (follow Procedure 3) |
| Presenting New Language: numbers 0–10 | Check Homework: check *bits and pieces envelopes* and *photos* | Check Homework: use Class Cassette, Unit 1, Part 3 | Check Homework: use Class Cassette Unit 1, Parts 3 and 4 |
| Action Game: use Class Cassette Unit 1, Part 10–12 (follow Procedure 1) | Presenting New Language: teach colours of eyes, hair and clothes | Presenting New Language: common classroom items | Unit 1 Workpage (Student's Book page 3): use Home Cassette Unit 1, Parts A and B |
| Game: play *Twister* with numbers | Activity: the children measure heights – record results on class chart | Activity: the children measure jumps and hops – record results on class chart | Language Practice: giving information about the results |
| Review: the children say how old they are | Language Practice: giving short, true answers about the results | Language Practice: giving short, true answers about the results | Homework: finish off Unit 1 Workpage (Student's Book page 3) |
| Homework: glue in a *bits and pieces* envelope; bring in a passport photo | Homework: do the other measuring activities on Unit 1 Activity Page | Homework: complete and tidy up Activity Page (Student's Book page 2) | Round Up: the children sing *One little indian* – use Class Cassette Unit 1, Part 5 |
| Round Up: the children make numbers with their bodies | Round Up: writing numbers on a friend's back | Round Up: the children sing *One little indian* – use Class Cassette Unit 1, Part 5 | |

# Lesson 1
# Preparation Activities

## PREPARING YOUR LESSON

– Prepare simple flash cards for numbers 0–10.

– For demonstration purposes, glue an envelope onto the inside front cover of *early bird* and bring in a passport size photo of yourself.

## WARM UP

• group formation activity
• learning some of the names

Play *Chinese whispers* with the children's names. Ask the children to sit in a circle. Whisper one of the children's names to S1. The children pass the name round the circle by whispering. The last child says the name. The child with that name stands up and begins the next 'whisper'.

## PRESENTING NEW LANGUAGE

• active understanding of numbers 0–10
• building the children's confidence
• learning everyone's names
• group formation activity

Numbers: 0–10. Use flashcards of the numbers as teaching aids.

i. Organise the class into a semi-circle. Give out the flash cards of the numbers (at random) to the children, making one child responsible for one number. You say the number as you give out the card. The children listen only.

ii. You say the numbers. The children hold up the appropriate flash card. They don't speak.
T: *This is number 1.*
*This is number 2 . . . etc.*

iii. The children exchange numbers. You say the numbers. The class points to the appropriate flash card. They don't speak.
T: *Point to number 1.*
*Point to number 5 . . . etc.*

iv. Ask the children to put their number flash cards in various locations in the classroom. Organise the class into groups of three or four. Ask groups to stand near specific number flash cards. You then say the numbers. Groups put their hands up when they hear their number. They don't speak.
T: *David and Julia, stand next to number 5, over there. Pepe and Teresa, stand here, next to number*

7 *. . . etc. Now, who's standing near number 6? Put your hands up . . . Hands down. Now who's standing near number 3? Hands up . . . Hands down . . . etc.*

v. Ask the children to move to a new number flash card of their choice. You say the numbers. This time the children say their names when they hear their number.
T: *Number 6.*
Ss: *Marti, Maria, Margherita.*
T: *Number 8.*
Ss: *Ana, Pepe, Barbara . . . etc.*

vi. Ask the children to move to another new number of their choice. You say the numbers. The children say their names when they hear their number. After each child says his or her name, the rest of the class repeats the name (in a whisper or loud voice depending on your classroom neighbours). Continue until all the children have had their names repeated by the class.
T: *Number 6.*
S1: *Maria.*
Ss: *MARIA.*
S2: *Margherita.*
Ss: *MARGHERITA . . . etc.*

vii. Ask the children to stand in a circle. You choose one number flash card. You walk around the group with this number flash card and teach it to various children. You encourage all the children to do the same with the numbers they are holding.
T–S1: *Four.*
S1–T: *Eight.*
T–S2: *Four.*
S2–T: *One.*
S1–S3: *Eight.*
S3–S1: *Six.*
S2–S5: *One.*
S5–S2: *Seven . . . etc.*
You move into the background as this activity gathers momentum. Encourage the children to help and correct each other.

viii. *Consolidation steps:*
– You stop the activity. You say each of the numbers. The children hold their flash cards above their heads when they hear their number. The children then exchange flash cards, and repeat the above activity.
– Each child holds a number, or joins children who are holding a number. You ask the children to stand in a line, in numerical order. When they are in a line, encourage them to count off the numbers in numerical order, starting with zero.
S1, S2 + S3: *Zero.*
S4 + S5: *One.*
S6, S7 + S8: *Two . . . etc.*

– The children exchange numbers, re-organise themselves into the correct numerical order and repeat the activity.

ix. As a finale, all the children shout (or whisper) their numbers in unison.

The above procedure takes between 15 and 20 minutes. The children are involved the whole time. The activity starts with the children taking responsibility for recognising one word only. By the time the activity ends, all the children will have had the chance to teach each other all the words.

## ACTION GAME

- active understanding of important classroom language
- introducing the routine for Action Games
- developing confidence
- providing a physical response experience of language

Use Unit 1, Part 1 on the Class Cassette. This is the first time the children have played this game, so follow Action Game Procedure 1.

## Procedure 1

i. You play the Cassette and demonstrate the actions. The children listen and watch only (no speaking).

ii. Play the Cassette again. You and the children do the actions together. The children don't speak.

iii. Play the Cassette again. You watch the children. The children do the actions (no speaking). Help with mime only if there are problems.

*Tapescript*
*Unit 1, Part 1. Listen and do the actions.*
Put your hand up. Put your hand down.
Stand up. Come here. Go over there. Sit down.

*Note:* Class size and classroom layout are important factors for Physical Response Activities. If the desks and chairs are movable, make the first step of the Action Game a series of *moving furniture* instructions. (Later on in the course, encourage the children to give these themselves.) In a more traditional classroom setting, and with large classes, create a demonstration space in the classroom. Ask groups to demonstrate, and get the remainder of the class to comment on performance. In all events, the Action Game can be adapted to suit your classroom environment.

## GAME

Play *Twister* with numbers 0–10.

*Rules*
The children receive instructions to touch the numbers with various parts of their bodies. For example:

T: *Touch number 4 with your left hand. Now, touch number 6 with your right elbow. Now, touch number 8 with your left knee. OK let go of number 4 and touch number 9 with your left hand . . . etc.*

The children must keep touching all the numbers until asked otherwise. Those who fall over or fail to touch, are out of the game or lose a team point.

i. Organise the class into groups of five. Ask groups to write numbers 0–9 on pieces of paper. In this way, each group should produce ten numbers.

ii. Ask the groups to pick up their numbers and put them on desk tops or the floor. Make sure that the numbers are reasonably close together for the game.

iii. Demonstrate how to play with S1 and S2. Use lots of gesture to explain the parts of the body you want the children to use.

iv. Play the game.

## REVIEW

Review activity for numbers 0–10: find out how old the children are. Use the 'happy birthday' tune or a drawing of a birthday cake to explain your question.

T: *How old are you Mariko?*
S: *Nine.*
T: *How old are you, Toni? . . . etc.*

Record ages on a simple column chart on the board. Find out who are the oldest and youngest in the class.

## HOMEWORK

Ask the children to glue a *bits and pieces* envelope onto the inside front cover of the book. Also ask them to bring in a passport size photo of themselves for the next lesson.

## ROUND UP

- reviewing numbers
- group formation activity

The children make numbers with their bodies. Organise the children into groups of five or six. You say or show a number. The groups form the shape of that number, for example, by standing and linking arms. Demonstrate with one group first, moving bodies and joining the group to explain the meaning of the activity to the children. Give lots of encouragement and praise for imaginative shapes. End the activity with the number 8 which is to be formed by the whole class linking arms or hands.

# Lesson 2
# Measuring (1)

## PREPARING YOUR LESSON

– Bring in at least two tape measures.

– Complete 50% of your own Unit 1 Activity Page (Student's Book page 2) for demonstration purposes.

– Prepare a simple *column chart* on the board or a large sheet of paper to record the children's heights.

– Bring in spare envelopes in case any children forget their *bits and pieces* envelopes.

## WARM UP

• introducing the key actions for the measuring activity, for example: *reach up, stretch, stand, hop, jump*
• group formation activity

Use the Action Game on the Class Cassette (Unit 1, Part 2). This is the first time the children have played this Action Game, so follow Action Game Procedure 1 on page 15.

O – 24

*Tapescript*
*Unit 1, Part 2. Listen and do the actions.*
Reach up with your arms. Higher. Higher. Relax.
Now stretch your arms out. Wider. Wider. Relax.
Now. Right foot. Stand on your right foot, and hop.
1 . . . 2 . . . 3 . . . hop.
Left foot. Stand on your left foot. 1 . . . 2 . . . 3 . . . hop.
Now both feet. 1 . . . 2 . . . 3 . . . jump.
Now curl up. Really small. Smaller. Smaller. Relax.

## CHECK HOMEWORK

Check that all the children have glued an envelope onto the inside front cover of the book. Get the children to show you the photos they have brought in. Ask the children to glue their photos onto page 2 of their *early bird* books.
*Note*: It is very probable that some children will not have done the homework. In practical terms this may mean giving out envelopes and gluing them in as a class activity. Do insist that homework is taken seriously by all the children. Even a small homework task will encourage the children to review classwork at home.

## PRESENTING NEW LANGUAGE

• active understanding of basic colours
• building the children's confidence
• group formation activity

Teach the common colours for eyes, hair and clothes. For example: *brown, blue, green*. Ask the children to colour small sheets of paper with their crayons, and use these as teaching aids. Use a similar procedure to the one used in Lesson 1.

i. After the children have coloured in their sheets of paper, organise the class into a semi-circle.

ii. You say the colours. The children hold them up. They don't speak.

iii. The children exchange colours. You say the colours. The children must touch something (other than the coloured sheet of paper) of that colour. They don't speak.

iv. Play *Twister* with the colours. Refer back to Lesson 1 of this Unit for the procedure.

18/1/94 Write colours a learn

v. Ask the children to stand in a circle. You choose the colours of your eyes, hair and clothes. Walk around the group teaching these colours to various children. You encourage all the children to teach classmates the colour of their eyes, hair and clothes. Draw face & write. - I've got brown eyes and brown hair. Draw jumper + trousers.

vi. *Consolidation step*: You stop the activity. You say each of the colours. Then you ask the children questions about the colour of your and their hair, eyes and clothes.

vii. Divide the class into two teams. S1 from each team stands in front of your desk. You display some colours. Allow the two children five seconds to look at the colours then ask them to close their eyes. You remove or add one colour. The children open their eyes. The first to say or find an example of the missing or extra colour scores a team point. Continue until all the children have had a turn. Repeat this activity with the children working in pairs.

## ACTIVITY

- teaching measuring skills
- encouraging the children to estimate heights
- encouraging the children to compare heights
- investigating relationship (if any) between height and age, height and sex, height and reach, stretch, foot size, etc.
- encouraging the children to use the following words and expressions: *yes/no, me, him, her, numbers, units (centimetres)*

24/1/94

i. If necessary, teach the skills of measuring accurately with a tape measure:
   - Give S1 and S2 a tape measure each. Ask what the first number on the scale is. Ask what the last number is. Ask other children to confirm this. Teach the word *centimetre.*
     T: *What's the first number on the scale?*
     S1: *Zero.*
     T: *What's the last number?*
     S2: *One, five, zero.*
     T: *What is this called? Anybody know?*
     S3(+T): *Centimetre.*
   - Choose three children. Ask S1 and S2 to measure S3. Write up the result.
   - Elicit and demonstrate other good and bad ways of measuring. The children choose the best way.

ii. Start the measuring activity. The children work in groups of three. Before starting the activity, check that all the children have everything they need.
   - The children measure their heights. In a large class, get the groups to take turns. For example, two groups at a time use the tape measures. They write up the results on the board.

## LANGUAGE PRACTICE

- encouraging the children to give true answers to questions about height
- active understanding of a range of question forms

Ask questions about height, comparison of height, etc. Use gesture to explain your meaning where necessary. For example:

T: *Stand in a line. Who's the tallest? Hands up. Who's the tallest, Ken?*
S: *Maria.*
T: *How tall are you, Maria?*
S: *One, four, seven centimetres.*
T: *How tall are you, Toni?*
S: *One, three, eight centimetres.*
T: *Who's the shortest? . . . etc.*

*Note:* The children express their height in single numbers.

## HOMEWORK

Ask the children to complete at home the remaining measurements (except hop and jump) shown on page 2 of their *early bird* books. Show and explain what to do by using your own completed page 2 as a model.

## ROUND UP

- group formation activity
- review of numbers
- friendship activity

25/1/94

Writing numbers on a partner's back.

i. Organise the children into a semi-circle. Choose S1. You stand or sit behind S1 and write a number on his or her back with your finger. S1 must then guess the number and write it (with his or her finger) on the palm of your hand. Change roles and repeat.

ii. Organise the class into pairs. Pairs do the *writing numbers* activity. Change partners and repeat this activity several times.

iii. Organise the class into two team lines. The lines stand facing the board.

iv. Write a number on the backs of the two children at the end of their team lines. The children pass the number towards the front child in the line by writing it on the back of the next child in the line. The front child writes the number on the board. The first team to finish is allowed to leave the class first.

# Lesson 3
# Measuring (2)

## PREPARING YOUR LESSON

– Prepare a selection of important classroom items, for example: *pencil, eraser, glue, crayon, etc.*

– Bring in some bathroom scales.

– Prepare a *results table* on the board or a large piece of paper to record potential results of the children's measuring activities.

## WARM UP

- focusing on listening skills with respect to key words in the Action Game text
- giving further experience of the key action vocabulary in this Unit
- giving the children the confidence to give instructions in English

Use the Action Game on the Class Cassette (Unit 1, Part 2). This is the second time the children have played this game, so follow Action Game Procedure 2. The complete script may be too long to use at this stage for beginner level students. If so, use the first few instructions only.

## Procedure 2

i.  You play/say the complete script. The children do the actions (no speaking). You watch them.

ii. Organise the class into pairs. S1 of each pair takes the teaching role. S2 takes the acting role. Select a sequence of two or three instructions from the Action Game. You mime *action prompts* for each instruction. S1 from each pair attempts to say the instruction after each prompt. S2 does the actions (no speaking). Don't expect the children to give complete or accurate instructions at this stage. Don't correct errors. Encourage the children to do the best they can. After the children have tried, you play/say the Action lines again to the whole class – they listen. Pairs then change roles, and then partners, and repeat the activity. Once again, don't expect the children to give complete or accurate instructions. Encourage the children. Don't correct errors at this stage.

iii. You repeat the Action lines to the class – they listen. The class then gives you the instructions. You do the actions.

*Tapescript*
*Unit 1, Part 2. Listen and do the actions.*
Reach up with your arms. Higher. Higher. Relax.
Now stretch your arms out. Wider. Wider. Relax.
Now. Right foot. Stand on your right foot, and hop.
1 . . . 2 . . . 3 . . . hop.
Left foot. Stand on your left foot. 1 . . . 2 . . . 3 . . . hop.
Now both feet. 1 . . . 2 . . . 3 . . . jump.
Now curl up. Really small. Smaller. Smaller. Relax.

## CHECK HOMEWORK

i.  Draw or put up your results table on the board.

ii. Get the children to write the results of their homework measuring activities on this table.

iii. Ask them questions about the results. Use Unit 1, Part 3 on the Class Cassette. If the children have not weighed themselves, ask them to do so on the bathroom scales you have brought in.

*Tapescript*  0-9
*Unit 1, Part 3. Listen and give true answers.*
1. How old are you?
2. How tall are you?
3. How much do you weigh?
✗ 4. How long is your foot?

## PRESENTING NEW LANGUAGE

Teach the common classroom items, for example: *pencil, eraser, glue, crayon, etc.* Use real items as teaching aids. Use a similar presentation procedure to the one used in Lesson 1.

i.  Organise the class into a semi-circle. Give out the items to the children. You name the item as you give it to a child. They don't repeat it at this stage.

ii. You name the items. The children hold them up. They don't speak.
    T: *This is a ruler. This is a blue crayon . . . etc.*

iii. The children exchange items. You name the items. The child with the item holds it up. The remainder of the class does an action that represents the use of the item. They don't speak.

iv. Ask the children to put their items in various locations in the classroom. Organise the class into groups of three or four. Ask groups to stand by their item and touch it. You then name the items. Groups hold up their item. They don't speak.
    T: *Who's touching the glue? Hold it up . . . Put it down . . . etc.*
    children go to an item
    You name it
    child hold it up

v. Ask groups to exchange items. You then name the items. The appropriate group holds up the item. The remainder of the class calls out the names of the children in that group.
T: *Who's touching a red crayon?*
Class: *Marti, Maria, Margherita . . . etc.*

vi. Ask the children to stand in a circle. You choose one item. Walk around the group with this item, teaching it to various children. You encourage all the children to find their own item and teach classmates its English name. For example:
T–S1: *Glue.*
S1–T: *Pencil.*    ~~children teach each other~~
S1–S3: *Pencil.*
S3–S1: *Crayons . . . etc.*
You move into the background as this activity gathers momentum. Encourage the children to help and correct each other.

vii. *Consolidation step:* You stop the activity. You name each of the items. The children listen only. The children then exchange items and repeat the activity.

viii. Divide the class into two teams. S1 from each team stands in front of your desk. You display the items. Allow the two children five seconds to look at the items then ask them to close their eyes. You remove one item. The children open their eyes. The first to say or draw the missing item scores a team point. Continue until all the children have had a turn. Repeat this activity with the children working in pairs.

~~photocopier Timesaver p 70 cut & label.~~

## ACTIVITY

- reviewing and improving measuring skills
- encouraging the children to estimate distance
- investigating the relationship (if any) between height and ability to hop and jump
- encouraging the children to use the following words and expressions: *yes/no, me, him, her, numbers, units (centimetres)*

If appropriate, teach the skills of measuring *hopping and jumping* distance accurately and fairly with a tape measure. Get consensus on the best and fairest way to do this.

i. Start the measuring activity. The children work in groups of three. Before starting, check that all the children have everything they need.

ii. The children measure how far they can hop and jump. In a large class, divide the class into groups of four or five. Each group elects one child to hop and jump. Others are elected to measure the distance and S1 from each group is chosen to write up the results on the board.

## LANGUAGE PRACTICE

- giving true answers to questions about distance
- reviewing question forms (understanding only)

i. Ask how far the children hopped and jumped. Find out who hopped and jumped the furthest. Find out, for example, if the tallest children also hopped and jumped the furthest. Use gestures to explain your meaning where necessary. For example:
T: *How far did you hop, Mariko?*
S1: *One, six, one centimetres.*
T: *Who hopped the furthest?*
S2: *Me . . . etc.*

ii. Use Unit 1, Part 4 on the Class Cassette. Encourage the children to listen for key words in the questions. You want short, true answers only.

*Tapescript*
*Unit 1, Part 4. Listen and give true answers.*
1. How high can you reach?
2. How far can you stretch?
3. How high can you jump?
4. How far can you hop?

## HOMEWORK

Ask the children to complete and tidy up page 2 of their *early bird* books. Show your own book for demonstration purposes.

## ROUND UP

i. Teach *One little indian* using Unit 1, Part 5 on the Class Cassette.

ii. Divide the class into two teams. Teams stand in two lines facing each other. Team 1 sings with the Cassette. Assign a number from 1 to 10 to each of the children in Team 2. The children in Team 2 bob their heads when they hear their numbers in the song.

*Tapescript*
*Unit 1, Part 5. Listen and join in.*
One little, two little, three little indians . . .
Four little, five little, six little indians . . .
Seven little, eight little, nine little indians . . .
Ten little indian girls.

# Lesson 4
# Follow Up Activities

## PREPARING YOUR LESSON

– Complete your own Unit 1 Workpage (Student's Book page 3) for demonstration purposes.

## WARM UP

- giving further experience of the key action vocabulary in this Unit
- encouraging the children to give the first two instructions of the Action Game to a partner

Use the Action Game on the Class Cassette (Unit 1, Part 2). This is the third time the children have played this game, so follow Action Game Procedure 3.

## Procedure 3

i. You play/say the complete script. The class does the actions (no speaking). You watch the children.

ii. Divide the class into groups of three or four. Choose one leader per group. You play/say (softly) the Action Game script. Leaders repeat with (not after) you or the Cassette. Don't correct errors at this stage. The remaining children in the groups do the actions (no speaking).

iii. Change leaders. Repeat the activity without playing/saying the Action lines. You go round the groups helping if necessary. Whenever feasible, say the complete script while the children are listening. Then let them try. Encourage student-to-student correction rather than allowing the children merely to repeat line by line after you.

*Tapescript*
*Unit 1, Part 2. Listen and do the actions.*
Reach up with your arms. Higher. Higher. Relax.
Now stretch your arms out. Wider. Wider. Relax.
Now. Right foot. Stand on your right foot, and hop. 1 . . . 2 . . . 3 . . . hop.
Left foot. Stand on your left foot. 1 . . . 2 . . . 3 . . . hop.
Now both feet. 1 . . . 2 . . . 3 . . . jump.
Now curl up. Really small. Smaller. Smaller. Relax.

Encourage the children to give as many of the instructions as possible, without causing frustration. If the complete script is still too long to use at this stage, use the first few instructions only.

## CHECK HOMEWORK

i. Ask the children to open their books at Unit 1. Check that they have completed page 2.

ii. Review the results of the activity. Use Unit 1, Parts 3 and 4 on the Class Cassette.

*Tapescript* Children describe themselves
Who's the tallest/smallest
has the longest foot?
*Unit 1, Part 3. Listen and give true answers.*
1. How old are you?
2. How tall are you?
3. How much do you weigh?
4. How long is your foot?

*Unit 1, Part 4. Listen and give true answers.*
1. How high can you reach?
2. How far can you stretch?
3. How high can you jump?
4. How far can you hop?

## WORKPAGE

- showing the children how to complete their Workpages and use their Home Cassette
- reviewing language studied so far in this Unit
- focusing on listening skills

Demonstrate how to complete the Workpage, Student's Book page 3.

i. Show your own *early bird* book:
   – Turn to page 3. Show how you have completed it.
   – Check that the children understand the picture code instructions.

ii. Show the children the Home Cassette. Use this Cassette and complete Unit 1, Parts A and B with the class.

*Tapescript*
*Unit 1, Part A. Listen. Write your answers. Draw the pictures.*
1. How old are you?
2. How tall are you?
3. How much do you weigh?
4. How long is your foot?

*Unit 1, Part B. Listen. Write your answers. Colour in the pictures.*
1. How high can you reach?
2. How far can you stretch?
3. How high can you jump?
4. How far can you hop?

## LANGUAGE PRACTICE

Encourage the children to talk about the results of their measuring.

i.  You give the model. Use lots of gestures as you speak. For example:
    T: *I'm one, seven, four centimetres tall. I can hop one, zero, nine centimetres. I can jump two, four, three centimetres.*

ii. You repeat your information, leaving out key words. The class says the missing words.
    T: *I'm one, seven, four . . . . . . . . .*
    Ss: *Centimetres tall.*
    T: *I can . . . . . . . . . one, zero, nine . . . . . . . . .*
    Ss: *Hop . . . etc.*

iii. S1 comes to the front of the class. S1 gestures his or her height, hop and jump measurements (no speaking). The class describes them. Repeat this activity with a new S1.

iv. Organise the children into groups of three or four. The children take turns to describe measurements to their group. You go round and help with the language. Whenever feasible say a complete description while the children are listening. Then let them try. Encourage student-to-student correction rather than allowing the children merely to repeat line by line after you.

v.  Choose and encourage the children to describe their results to the rest of the class. Allow errors. Don't correct the children as they speak. Encourage all attempts. If needed, when a child has finished, repeat your own measurements. Get the other children to try.

## HOMEWORK

Assign page 3, Part C of the *early bird* book for homework. Encourage the children to ask their parents to sign their completed Workpage.

## ROUND UP

Review the song on the Class Cassette: *One little indian.*

*Tapescript*
*Unit 1, Part 5. Listen and join in.*
One little, two little, three little indians . . .
Four little, five little, six little indians . . .
Seven little, eight little, nine little indians . . .
Ten little indian girls.

## EVALUATION

• evaluating informally what the children have learned

In terms of evaluation of this Unit, the following table can be used as a guide. You may photocopy and include it in your school record book. For simplicity, tick a column if you are satisfied with a child's performance; leave it blank if you are not happy. *Note:* The table is a guide, and a record to refer back to. It is not intended as a grade list.

| Name | Activity completed | Can give the PR instructions for this Unit | Can understand your questions about measuring | Can give true responses | Can communicate information about height, etc. |
|------|------|------|------|------|------|
| | | | | | |
| | | | | | |
| | | | | | |
| | | | | | |
| | | | | | |
| | | | | | |
| | | | | | |

# Unit 2    Displaying Photos

## INTRODUCTION

This Unit asks the children to make a photo display on the Activity Page (Student's Book page 4) of any of the following:

– personal photos of family and pets;

– cartoon cut-outs of families (e.g. Mickey Mouse's family);

– photos or cut-outs of famous families.

Through the practical activities in Unit 2, the children will:

– learn how to display a range of photos neatly;

– state family relationships;

– use *family* vocabulary;

– use *numbers 0–20;*

– consolidate their active recognition of a wide range of question forms in English.

Table 1 (below) summarises the content of the Unit. Table 2 gives an outline of the key teaching steps.

Table 1

| The Children's Experience of Language Input across the Curriculum | | | Language Output from the Children in an Activity-Based Context | |
| --- | --- | --- | --- | --- |
| Activities and topics | Teacher's questions, instructions, and comments about: | Physical Response Activities | Vocabulary | Expressions and structures |
| displaying photos and cartoon pictures | family and family photos; neatness and display skills | stand over there stand back smile say | *family members* *pets* numbers 11–20 my your his her | taller than . . . smaller than . . . older than . . . younger than . . .<br><br>This is . . . Who's this . . . ? Is this . . . ? I'm . . . He's/She's . . . Maria's . . . (possessive s) |

**Table 2**

| Lesson 1<br>Preparation Activities | Lesson 2<br>Main Activity:<br>Displaying Photos | Lesson 3<br>Follow Up Activities |
|---|---|---|
| Warm Up: play *Who changed places?* | Warm Up: play *Who changed hats?*; Action Game: use Class Cassette Unit 2, Part 2 (follow Procedure 2) | Warm Up: Action Game: use Class Cassette Unit 2, Part 2 (follow Procedure 3) |
| Check Homework: review of numbers; colour *star* 1 in *star chart* | Check Homework: sort and display cartoon pictures of families into sets | Check Homework and Review: check photo display – use Class Cassette Unit 2, Part 4 |
| Presenting New Language: family vocabulary, pets | Presenting New Language: numbers 11–20 | Unit 2 Workpage (Student's Book page 5): use Home Cassette, Unit 2, Parts A, B and C |
| Action Game: use Class Cassette Unit 2, Part 2 (follow Procedure 1) | Activity: the children sort and display photos and cartoons onto Unit 2 Activity Page (Student's Book page 4) | Language Practice: identifying family |
| Review: play *Twister* with family flash cards | Language Practice: answering questions on family – use Class Cassette Unit 2, Part 3 | Game: play *Family bingo* |
| Homework: the children bring in cartoon pictures of families | Game: play *Happy families* | Homework: finish off Workpage activities (Student's Book page 5); bring in dice for next lesson |
| Round Up: take a class photo | Homework: finish gluing the pictures and photos onto the Activity Page; bring in four family pictures | Round Up: the children sing *One two, buckle my shoe* – use Class Cassette, Unit 2, Part 5 |
|  | Round Up: the children sing *One little indian* – use Class Cassette Unit 1, Part 5 |  |

# Lesson 1
# Preparation Activities

## PREPARING YOUR LESSON

The family is potentially a very sensitive area. To avoid embarrassment, find and use cartoon families taken from popular children's comics, or magazines. Alternatively use pictures of famous families.

- Make picture flash cards of members of the family with the cartoon pictures. Bring in your own family photos, if available.

- Complete your own Unit 1 pages. Have crayons (e.g. yellow and blue) available for the *star chart*.

## WARM UP

- group formation activity
- introducing the photo aspect of the theme of this Unit
- encouraging accurate observation
- reviewing the names of the children

Play *Who changed places?* Choose a group of children. Choose S1. S1 closes eyes. The group stands in a line. S1 opens eyes for five seconds and looks carefully at the group. S1 closes eyes. Two children in the group exchange places. S1 opens eyes, and guesses who moved. Change S1 and repeat the activity.

## CHECK HOMEWORK

- encouraging the children to evaluate their own work and other children's work
- showing the children how the *star chart* page works
- consolidating language from Unit 1

i. Show your completed pages for Unit 1. Ask the children what colour (grade) you deserve for your work. For example, yellow or blue? Use gestures to demonstrate that one colour means *fantastic* and the other means *OK*. Turn to the *star chart* on the inside back cover of the book. Abide by the class decision on your grade, and colour in *star 1* on the star chart.

ii. Ask the children to work in pairs. The children colour in their partner's *star* for this Unit. If there is any dispute, ask another child to be the final judge of grade. *Note:* The aim is to motivate the children to take pride in their work, not to penalise them for their lack of ability.

iii. Check that parents have signed their children's Workpage. In all events encourage children to share their work with their families.

## REVIEW

Review Unit 1.

i. Ask review questions about the results of Unit 1. Use Unit 2, Part 1 on the Class Cassette. Use gestures to explain the meaning of the question if needed.

*Tapescript*
*Unit 2, Part 1. Listen and answer. Point to the right person each time.*
1. Who's the tallest in the class?
2. Who's the smallest?
3. Who has the longest foot?
4. Who can jump the highest?
5. Who can stretch the furthest?

ii. Divide the class into two teams. S1 from each team steps forward. You ask *tallest*, *smallest*, *longest* questions. First correct answer scores a team point. Continue till one team scores five points.

## PRESENTING NEW LANGUAGE

- teaching the members of the family: *mum, dad, etc.*
- active understanding of *my, your, her, his, 's (Maria's)*
- encouraging the children to help each other and correct each other's errors

Members of the family. Use flash cards of family members as teaching aids.

a) Presentation.

   i. Organise the class into a semi-circle. Give out the picture flash cards of the members of the family to the children, making one child responsible for one word. You say the words as you give out the cards. The children listen only.

ii. You say the words. The children hold up the appropriate flash card. They don't speak.
T: *This is Mickey. This is Mickey's wife. This is Mickey's mum . . . etc.*

iii. The children exchange pictures. You say the words. Ask the class to point to the correct pictures.
T: *Point to Minnie's dad. Now, point to Mickey's brother . . . etc.*

iv. Ask the children to put the flash cards around the walls of the classroom. Organise the class into groups of three or four. Ask groups to stand under specific flash cards. You then say the words. Groups touch their noses when they hear their word. They don't speak.
T: *David and Julia, stand under Minnie's grandma, over there. Pepe and Teresa, stand here, under Mickey's dad . . . etc. Now, who's standing under Minnie's sister? Touch your nose . . . Hands down . . . etc.*

v. Ask the children to move to a new flash card of their choice. You say the words. The children must pose like the cartoon animal on the flash card when they hear their word.

vi. Ask the children to stand in a circle. You choose one flash card. You walk around the group with this flash card and teach it to various children. You encourage all the children to do the same with the pictures they are holding.
T–S1: *This is Mickey's mum.*
S1–T: *Minnie's sister.*
T– S2: *This is Mickey's mum.*
S2–T: *Mickey's grandad.*
S1–S3: *Minnie's sister.*
S3–S1: *Mickey's brother . . . etc.*
You move into the background as this activity gathers momentum. Encourage the children to help and correct each other.

vii. *Consolidation step*: You stop the activity. You name each of the members of the family. The children listen only. The children then exchange flash cards and repeat the above activity.

b) Practice.

i. Ask the children to sit down in groups of three or four. Ask them to draw two members of their own family. They choose who to draw. Draw a member of your own family on the board as an example. While the children are drawing, go round and chat to them about their pictures.

ii. When the children have finished, encourage a question and answer practice. Sit with one group, show your own family photographs (or drawings) and demonstrate what to do.

iii. You reinforce the language by giving examples for the children to listen to. (They don't repeat immediately after you.)
T: *This is my dad. This is my brother. This is Mickey's brother. Your turn.*
S1: *(This is) my mum, my sister, me.*
T: *Who's this?*
S2: *My dad, my grandma.*
T: *Let me show you my family again. This is my dad. This is my brother. And show me your pictures. This is Toni's . . . ?*
S3: *Dad.*
T: *And this is . . . ?*
S1: *Ana's brother . . . etc.*

iv. The children practise in their groups. You go round and help where necessary. If you want to correct errors, don't ask the children to repeat immediately after you. Say the correct phrases or sentences to the group, leave the group, and let them teach each other. Return to the group later on and check on progress. Accept good tries rather than aiming for perfection.

## ACTION GAME

• active understanding of *taking a photo* language
• group formation activity

Use Unit 2, Part 2 on the Class Cassette. This is the first time the children have played this game, so follow Action Game Procedure 1 on page 15.

*Tapescript*
*Unit 2, Part 2. Listen and do the actions.*
Stand over there, please. Back a bit. Good. Now smile. Say cheese. Thank you.

B

## REVIEW

Play *Twister* with the flash cards or pictures of the members of the family.
Demonstrate how to play the game: choose one group of children to play. Put the flash cards on the floor. Give instructions to the group to touch various flash cards with parts of their bodies.

T: *Touch Mickey's dad with your right hand. Now touch Minnie's brother with your left knee. Keep your right hand on Mickey's dad. Now put your left hand on . . . etc.*

The children who fall over, or who can't keep all the parts of their body on the various flash cards, are out of the game. Get other groups of children to play the game. Encourage the children to give the *Twister* instructions.

## HOMEWORK

For next lesson, ask the children to bring in cartoon, magazine or their own pictures of family groups and pets. Also ask them to bring in their own glue and scissors if these items are in short supply in your classroom.

## ROUND UP

Ask all the children to sit up straight and to be quiet. Choose five or six children. Take their photo using the Action Game script for this Unit. The children can leave after you've taken their photos.

# Lesson 2
# Displaying Photos

## PREPARING YOUR LESSON

– Display your own photos or cartoon cut-outs on the Unit 2 Activity Page (Student's Book page 4) and complete your Workpage (Student's Book page 5) for demonstration purposes.

– Bring in lots of spare cartoon pictures and cut-outs of famous families.

– Make simple number flash cards for the numbers 11–20.

– Bring in hats and scarves for a *family* role play.

## WARM UP

• consolidating the key actions and expressions for taking a photo, for example: *stand over there; back a bit; smile; say cheese; please; thank you*
• group formation activity
• observation activity

i. Play *Who changed hats?* Give out the hats and scarves. Choose a photographer (S1). The children pose for a family photo. S1 looks carefully at the group for five seconds, then closes his or her eyes. Two children swap hats or scarves. S1 opens his or her eyes and guesses the change. Repeat this activity two or three times.

ii. Action Game. Use the Action Game on the Class Cassette (Unit 2, Part 2). This is the second time the children have played this game, so follow Action Game Procedure 2 on page 18.

*Tapescript*
*Unit 2, Part 2. Listen and do the actions.*
Stand over there, please. Back a bit. Good. Now smile. Say cheese. Thank you.

## CHECK HOMEWORK

The children show the family pictures, photos or cartoons they have brought in. Ask the class to sort them into sets of the various family members and pets. Make sure they keep back any photos which are personal and which they might not wish to share with the rest of the class.

## PRESENTING NEW LANGUAGE

- using numbers 11–20
- encouraging the children to help each other and correct each other's errors

Numbers: 11–20. Use flash cards of the numbers as teaching aids.

i.  Organise the class into a semi-circle. Give out the flash cards of the numbers (at random) to the children. You say the number as you give out the card. The children listen only.

ii. You say the numbers. The children hold up the appropriate flash card. They don't speak.
T: *This is number 11.*
*This is number 15 . . . etc.*

iii. The children exchange numbers. You say the numbers. The class points to the appropriate flash card. They don't speak.

iv. Ask the children to put their number flash cards in various locations in the classroom. Organise the class into groups of three or four. Ask groups to stand near specific number flash cards. You then say the numbers. Groups put their hands up when they hear their number. They don't speak.
T: *David and Julia, stand next to number 15, over there. Pepe and Teresa, stand here, next to number 17 . . . etc. Now, who's standing near number 16? Put your hands up . . . Hands down. Now, who's standing near number 13? Hands up . . . Hands down . . . etc.*

v.  Ask the children to move to a new number flash card of their choice. You say the numbers. The children must form the shape of their number as a group – with their arms, legs and bodies.

vi. Collect the numbers. Organise the class into groups of three or four. Ask the groups to decide secretly on any of the numbers. Group 1 has to form the shape of their number with their arms, legs and bodies. The rest of the class guesses the number. Continue the activity until all groups have had a turn.

vii. Ask the children to stand in a circle. You choose one number flash card. You walk around the group with this number flash card and teach it to various children. You encourage all the children to do the same with the numbers they are holding.
T–S1: *Fourteen.*
S1–T: *Eighteen.*
T–S2: *Fourteen.*
S2–T: *Eleven.*
S1–S3: *Eighteen.*
S3–S1: *Sixteen . . . etc.*

You move into the background as this activity gathers momentum. Encourage the children to help and correct each other.

viii. *Consolidation step:* You stop the activity. You say each of the numbers. The children listen only. The children then exchange flash cards and repeat the activity.

ix. Each child holds a number, or joins the children who are holding a number. You ask the children to stand in a line, in numerical order. When they are in a line, encourage them to count off the numbers in numerical order, starting with eleven.
S1, S2 + S3: *Eleven*
S4 + S5: *Twelve*
S6, S7 + S8: *Thirteen . . . etc.*
The children exchange numbers, re-organise themselves into the correct numerical order and repeat the activity.

x.  As a finale, all the children shout (or whisper) their numbers in unison.

*Copy out nos 11–20 from board to learn*

## ACTIVITY *cut out pics from catalogue to make a family & stick*

- consolidating *family* vocabulary
- sorting and displaying family pictures, cartoons and photos

i.  Organise the classroom and the children so that they can work in groups of four. Make sure there are lots of extra cartoon pictures for any children who have not got enough, and see that all groups have access to glue and scissors. Ask the children to glue their photos onto page 4 of their *early bird* books. You go round and help.

ii. Make sure the displays are neat. Praise neat work and interesting photos or pictures. Ask lots of relevant questions. Use gestures to explain the meaning of your questions where necessary.
T: *Who's this, Terri?*
S1: *My brother.*
T: *What's his name?*
S1: *Paulo.*
T: *How old is he?*
S1: *Five.*
T: *Is he taller than you?*
S1: *No.*
T: *Is this your cat?*
S2: *Yes.*
T: *What's your cat's name?*
S2: *Pepper.*
T: *What colour . . . ? etc.*

## LANGUAGE PRACTICE

- encouraging the children to answer questions about family
- active understanding of a range of *wh-* questions

Use Unit 2, Part 3 on the Class Cassette.

i.  Organise the children into groups of four. Sit with one group. Other groups observe. Look at S1's photos. Point to a photo and ask *wh-* questions.
    T: *Who's this?*
    S: *My dad.*
    T: *And who's this?*
    S: *My brother.*

ii. Choose a leader for each group. Play the Cassette. Pause the Cassette after each question, rewind and play the question again, encouraging the leaders to ask the questions with the Cassette.
    Group members answer. Don't correct errors at this stage.

    *Tapescript*
    *Unit 2, Part 3. Look at your friend's photos and ask these questions.*
    1. Who's this?
    2. And who's this?

iii. Change leaders. Repeat the activity without the Cassette.

## GAME

Play *Happy families*.

i.  Organise the children into groups of three or four. Each group chooses one cartoon character. They each do a quick drawing of one family member for this character on a small piece of paper.

ii. You collect in the original cartoon pictures and display them on the board or the wall.

iii. You collect in the children's drawings and mix them up. Using sellotape, you attach, at random, one drawing to the back of each child.

iv. The children line up against the wall, so that no-one can see the picture on anyone's back. Choose two family leaders (S1 and S2). Leaders come to the front of the class and turn round showing the pictures on their backs. The remaining children call out the leaders' identities. For example:
    Class: *You're Mickey's mum.*

v.  Leaders take turns to find their families by guessing the identity of the children lined up against the wall. When their names are called out, the children turn round to reveal their identity. The first leader to get three 'relations' wins.
    S1: *Are you Mickey's dad?*

## HOMEWORK

Ask the children to finish off their photo displays on page 4 of their *early bird* books. Ask them to bring four pictures of their family, or their favourite famous people, or cartoon characters. They will need these for the activities on the Workpage (Student's Book page 5). Use your own completed Workpage for demonstration purposes.

## ROUND UP

Review the song from Unit 1, Part 5 on the Class Cassette: *One little indian*. Refer back to Unit 1, Lesson 4 for the script and procedure.

# Lesson 3
# Follow Up Activities

## PREPARING YOUR LESSON

– Bring in lots of spare cut-outs of family groups.

## WARM UP

• group formation
• consolidating and using the language of the Action Game

Use the Action Game on the Class Cassette (Unit 2, Part 2). This is the third time the children have played this game, so follow Action Game Procedure 3 on page 20.

## CHECK HOMEWORK AND REVIEW

Check the photos and cut-outs that the children have brought in. Use your spares and make sure that all the children have four photos or pictures.

i. Organise the children into a semi-circle. Divide the semi-circle into two teams. Point to photos and pictures and ask 'Is this . . . (Donald's grandad)?' questions. The children answer yes or no. For example:
T: *Is this Scoobie's dad?*
S: *No . . . etc.*
Correct answers score a team point.

ii. Encourage the children to ask the questions. S1 from Team 1 asks the children from Team 2. Correct questions and answers score team points.

iii. Organise the children into groups of three or four. Each group chooses a leader. Play Unit 2, Part 4 on the Class Cassette. Pause the Cassette after each question, rewind and play the question again, encouraging the leaders to ask the questions with the Cassette. (Leaders must point to an appropriate photo or picture as they ask the question.) Group members answer. Don't correct errors at this stage.

*Tapescript*
*Unit 2, Part 4. Look at your friend's photos and ask similar questions to these.*
1. Is this your sister?
2. Is this your friend?

iv. The children change roles, then groups and repeat the activity. You go round and encourage the children. Help with the language if necessary. Encourage them to make up their own questions.

## WORKPAGE

• showing the children how to use their Home Cassette at home

a) Complete the Workpage, Student's Book page 5. Use Unit 2, Parts A, B and C on the Home Cassette. Demonstrate how to do Part A, the *Teach your parents* activity at home[1]. For example: do a role play for the *Teach your parents* situation. Choose two children. S1 is the parent. S2 is him- or herself.

i. Give a short practical demonstration on how to use the cassette player.

ii. Role play: S2 plays the Cassette and demonstrates the actions on the Cassette. S1 (the parent) watches and listens.

iii. S2 plays the Cassette again and does the actions with the parent.

iv. S2 gives the instructions with the Cassette. The parent does the actions. S2 watches.

*Tapescript*
*Unit 2, Part A. Listen. Teach your parents. Stand over there, please. Back a bit. Good. Now smile. Say cheese. Thank you.*

b) Demonstrate how to do Parts B and C. Show your own Student's Book page 5. The children glue in four photos or pictures onto their page 5. When the children are ready:

i. Organise the class into pairs. You play the Cassette. Pause the tape after each question, rewind and play the question again, encouraging S1 to ask the questions with the Cassette. S2 answers. The children change roles, then partners and repeat the activity without the Cassette. You go round the class helping where necessary.

*Tapescript*
*Unit 2, Part B. Glue in your photos. Listen. Write in who it is.*
1. Who's this?
2. And who's this?

*Unit 2, Part C. Glue in your photos. Listen. Write yes or no.*
1. Is this your sister?
2. Is this your friend?

ii. You play the Cassette again, the children write the one word answers on page 5. Write the words on the board for the children to copy if necessary.

[1] This activity may be too difficult for younger children. With a younger class, you will need to do a higher percentage of the Workpage activities in class time.

## LANGUAGE PRACTICE

- giving the children the opportunity to use English to describe their photos or pictures
- consolidation of the language learned in this Unit

Encourage the children to talk about their photos.

i. You give an example. Point to your photos as you speak.
T: *This is my brother. He's nineteen. His name's Paul.*

ii. Organise the children into groups of three or four. The children take turns to describe their photos or pictures to their group. You go round and help with the language. Whenever feasible say a complete description while the children are listening. Then let them try. Encourage student-to-student correction rather than allowing the children merely to repeat line by line after you.

iii. Choose and encourage the children to talk about their photos to the rest of the class. Allow errors. Don't correct the children as they speak. For example:
S: *This is my brother. He's eight. His name's Ken.*
Encourage all attempts. If needed, when a child has finished, repeat your example. Get the other children to try.

## GAME

- reviewing family vocabulary
- focusing on listening skills

Play *Family bingo.*

i. Display a wide selection of cartoon family members, and famous people's family members.

ii. Ask the children to choose any three characters or people from your selection, and draw them (or write who they are) on a sheet of their own paper.

iii. You put the pictures into a bag or box. When the children are ready, you pick out pictures from the bag, and call them out. The children check their drawings as you call them. The first child to match his or her three drawings wins a prize (e.g. a sweet), and becomes the caller for a repeat game.

## HOMEWORK

Ask the children to tidy up pages 4 and 5 of their *early bird* books. Encourage the children to ask their parents to sign their completed Workpage. Also ask them to bring in one dice each for the next lesson.

## ROUND UP

Teach *One, two, buckle my shoe* using Unit 2, Part 5 on the Class Cassette. Encourage the children to use gestures as they sing.

*Tapescript*
*Unit 2, Part 5. Listen and join in.*
One, two, buckle my shoe.
Three, four, knock at the door.
Five, six, pick up sticks.
Seven, eight, put them straight.
Nine, ten, start again.

## EVALUATION

- evaluating informally what the children have learned

In terms of evaluation of this Unit, the following table can be used as a guide. You may photocopy and include it in your school record book. For simplicity, tick a column if you are satisfied with a child's performance; leave it blank if you are not happy.
*Note:* The table is a guide, and a record to refer back to. It is not intended as a grade list.

| Name | Activity completed | Can give the PR instructions for this Unit | Can understand your questions about the family | Can give true responses | Can communicate information about the family |
|---|---|---|---|---|---|
| | | | | | |
| | | | | | |
| | | | | | |
| | | | | | |

# Unit 3  Beetles

## INTRODUCTION

This Unit reviews language learned so far, and extends the children's knowledge in English of *numbers*, *adjectives* and *parts of the body*. The Unit focuses on the *number 3* and *Beetles*.

*Number 3:*
- adding threes;

- subtracting threes;

- multiplying by three;

- the shape of the number 3.

*Beetles:*
- the game Beetle;

- making a model beetle;

- main parts of the body of a model beetle;

- observing and describing *mini-beasts*.

Through the practical activities in Unit 3, the children:

- play number games in English;

- work together and make a large model beetle;

- teach each other *simple arithmetic* in English;

- use *parts of the body* vocabulary;

- use *numbers* 0–31;

- use *have/has* to describe their beetles;

- use *adjectives* to describe their beetles;

- consolidate their active recognition of a wide range of question forms in English.

Table 1 (below) summarises the content of the Unit. Table 2 gives an outline of the key teaching steps.

### Table 1

| The Children's Experience of Language Input across the Curriculum | | | Language Output from the Children in an Activity-Based Context | |
| --- | --- | --- | --- | --- |
| Activities and topics | Teacher's questions, instructions, and comments about: | Physical Response Activities | Vocabulary | Expressions and structures |
| beetles, beetle games; number games | making a beetle; playing beetle; numbers and simple arithmetic | draw throw cut glue pick say | *parts of the body* numbers 21–31 long big little round dice a/the | my turn your turn his turn her turn It has (got) . . . |

**Table 2**

| Lesson 1 Preparation Activities | Lesson 2 Main Activity: Making a Beetle | Lesson 3 Follow Up Activities |
|---|---|---|
| Warm Up: writing numbers on a friend's back | Warm Up: Action Game: use Class Cassette Unit 3, Part 1 (follow Procedure 2) | Warm Up: Action Game: use Class Cassette Unit 3, Part 2 (follow Procedure 3) |
| Check Homework: colour *star 2* in *star chart*; review numbers; number work with dice | Presenting New Language: parts of the beetle's body | Check Homework: look at completed Activity Page (Student's Book page 6) |
| Presenting New Language: numbers 21–31 | Check Homework: sort the materials brought in | Review and Language Practice: play *Team beetle* |
| Action Game: use Class Cassette Unit 3, Part 1 (follow Procedure 1) | Activity: the children make a giant beetle out of card, paper and scrap materials | Language Practice: the children talk about their beetles |
| Activity: play *Buzz 3* | Review: the children sing *One, two, buckle my shoe* – use Class Cassette Unit 2, Part 5 | Unit 3 Workpage (Student's Book page 7): use Home Cassette, Unit 3, Parts A, B and C |
| Game: play *Bingo* with numbers | Homework: bring in pictures of real beetles | Homework: observation and drawing of mini-beasts |
| Homework: the children bring in a range of *junk* materials | Round Up: play story game with *numbers* and *colours* | Round Up: the children sing *Head, body, legs and tail* – use Class Cassette, Unit 3, Part 5 |
| Round Up: the children sing *One, two, buckle my shoe* – use Class Cassette Unit 2, Part 5 | | |

# Lesson 1
# Preparation Activities

## PREPARING YOUR LESSON

- Prepare number flash cards for the numbers 21–31.
- For demonstration purposes, bring in a sample of *junk* materials (e.g. scraps of wool, coloured paper, buttons) of the type needed for making a *giant beetle* in Lesson 2 of this Unit.

## WARM UP

- group formation activity
- reviewing and consolidating numbers
- friendship activity

Writing numbers on a partner's back.

i. Demonstrate the activity with S1. You sit behind S1 and write a number on his or her back with your finger. S1 must guess the number and write it on the palm of your hand. You change roles and repeat the activity.

ii. Organise the children into pairs. S1 sits behind S2. Pairs do the finger writing activity.

iii. The children change roles, then partners and repeat the activity.

## CHECK HOMEWORK

- encouraging the children to evaluate their own work and other children's work
- consolidating language from Unit 2
- motivating the children to bring in dice next lesson

i. Show your completed pages for Unit 2. As for Unit 1, ask the children what colour (grade) you deserve for your work. For example, yellow or blue? Use gestures to demonstrate that one colour means *fantastic* and the other means *OK*. Turn to the *star chart* on the inside back cover of the book. Abide by the class decision on your grade, and colour in *star 2* on the star chart.

ii. Ask the children to work in pairs. The children colour in their partner's *star* for this Unit. If there is any dispute, ask another child to be the final judge of grade.

iii. Check that parents have signed their children's Workpage.

iv. Find out how many children have brought in dice. Take two dice. Ask the children to predict the scores when you throw the dice. Make a simple chart on the board.

| Throw | Score | Throw | Score |
|-------|-------|-------|-------|
| 1 | | 11 | |
| 2 | | 12 | |
| 3 | | 13 | |
| 4 | | 14 | |
| 5 | | 15 | |
| 6 | | 16 | |
| 7 | | 17 | |
| 8 | | 18 | |
| 9 | | 19 | |
| 10 | | 20 | |

v. Ask S1 to throw the two dice 20 times. Enter the score each time he or she throws the dice. Count the frequency of scores. Which score occurs most often? Why? Ask the children to add up in English the score possibilities for two dice. For example: *1 plus 1 equals 2; 1 plus 2 equals 3; 2 plus 2 equals 4; 3 plus 1 equals 4; 4 plus 1 equals 5; 2 plus 3 equals 5; 3 plus 3 equals 6; 2 plus 4 equals 6; 5 plus 1 equals 6; etc.*

vi. If you throw two dice 100 times, how many scores of 7 will there be? Note down who guessed what, to compare with their results next lesson. Ask the children to try this at home – and insist that all the children (especially those who have forgotten their dice this lesson) bring in one dice for the next lesson.

## PRESENTING NEW LANGUAGE

- numbers 21–31
- consolidating numbers already learned
- group formation activity

Numbers: 21–31. Use flash cards of the numbers as teaching aids.

i. Show your flash cards in random order to the children. Ask all the children to copy the number of their choice onto a blank piece of paper. When finished, the children put these into their pockets for later.

ii. Organise the class into a semi-circle. Give out the flash cards of the numbers (at random) to the children, making one child responsible for one number. You say the number as you give out the card. The children listen only.

iii. You say the numbers. The children hold up the appropriate flash card. They don't speak.

iv. You say the numbers. The children with the number flash cards hold them up. The remainder of the class shows the value of the number with their fingers. They don't speak at this stage.

v. Ask the children to put their number flash cards in various locations in the classroom. Organise the class into groups of three or four. Ask groups to stand near specific number flash cards. You then say the numbers. Groups must put both hands in the air when they hear their number. They don't speak.

vi. Ask the children to move to another number of their choice. You say the *twenty (or thirty)* part of the number, and point to a group. That group says the remainder.
T: *Twenty...*
G1: *Five.*
T: *Twenty...*
G2: *Nine... etc.*
Encourage the children to take your role. S1 says the *twenty* part of the number, and chooses a group to complete the number.

vii. Ask the children to stand in a circle. You choose one number flash card. You walk around the group with this number flash card and teach it to various children. You encourage all the children to do the same with the numbers they drew at the beginning of this activity.
T–S1: *Twenty-four.*
S1–T: *Twenty-eight.*
T–S2: *Twenty-four.*
S2–T: *Twenty-one... etc.*
You move into the background as this activity gathers momentum. Encourage the children to help and correct each other.

viii. *Consolidation step:* You stop the activity. You say each of the numbers. When the children hear their numbers, they hold them up. The children then exchange flash cards and repeat the activity.

ix. Each child holds a number, or joins children who are holding a number. You ask the children to stand in a line, in numerical order. When they are in a line, encourage them to count off the numbers in numerical order, starting with twenty-one. The children then exchange numbers, re-organise themselves into the correct numerical order and repeat the activity.

## ACTION GAME

- consolidation of classroom language
- group formation activity

i. Ask the children to write a number between 0 and 31 on a piece of paper before you start the activity. Collect in and display the numbers on an accessible desk.

ii. Use Unit 3, Part 1 on the Class Cassette. This is the first time the children have played this game, so follow the adapted Action Game Procedure 1 below:
   – You play the Cassette and demonstrate the actions. The children listen and watch only (no speaking).
   – Choose three or four children to do the actions. The remainder of the class observes. Play the Cassette again. You and the children do the actions together. The children say the numbers they pick up.
   – Choose new groups of children. Play the Cassette again. You watch the children. The children do the actions and say the numbers as they pick them up. Help with mime only if there are problems.

*Write down nos 21–31 e both*

**Tapescript** O – 10
*Unit 3, Part 1. Listen and do the actions.*
Ready? Stand up please. Come here. Pick up a number. Say the number. Put the number down. Sit down.

## ACTIVITY

- consolidation of numbers
- expressing simple maths sentences in English (also introducing the present simple tense)

a) Pre-teach the notion of working in *threes*.

   i. Teach the children the 3 times table in English. Ask simple multiplication questions. Write them up on the board. For example:
   $3 \times 5 = ...$
   $3 \times 8 = ...$
   $3 \times ... = 21$
   T: *3 times 5 equals...*
   S: *15.*
   T: *3 times 8...*
   S: *Equals 24.*
   T: *3...*
   S: *Times 7 equals 21.*

ii. Choose S1. S1 takes your role. S1 stands at the board and writes up an incomplete sum. The other children answer. Don't correct S1 while he or she is speaking. If there are errors, when he or she has finished, you have another turn at the board before asking a new student to be the teacher. For example:
S1: *3 time 7 equal . . . ?*
S2: *21.*
S1: *Good.*
T: *Thanks, Mariko, very good. My turn again. 3 times 5 equals 15. 3 times 8 equals . . . what, Yoshihiro? . . . etc.*

iii. Pairwork. S1 of each pair asks the 3 times table questions. S2 answers. You go round the class and help with the language if needed. As before, don't encourage the children merely to repeat after you. Give the children complete examples to listen to, leave the group, and allow them to practise. Return later to check on results.

b) Play *Buzz 3* (see Unit 3 Activity Page, Student's Book page 6).

### Rules

Players mustn't say the number 3, or multiple of 3, or any number in which there is a 3. They must say *Buzz* instead.

i. The children stand in a circle. S1 starts counting at zero. The children take it in turns to say a number. If a child makes a mistake, he or she is out of the game. The winner is the last one left. If a mistake is made, the next child starts counting again from zero.

ii. Play the game two or three times only. Then check or teach the 4 times table and play *Fizz 4.* Number 4 is the forbidden number. Follow the same rules: the children must say *Fizz* instead of *four.*

## GAME

* reviewing numbers
* focusing on listening skills

Play *Bingo* with numbers 0–31.

i. Divide the class into three groups. Ask Group 1 to write numbers 0–10 on small, separate pieces of paper. Ask Group 2 to write numbers 11–21, and Group 3 to write numbers 22–31. Collect in the pieces of paper and put them in a box or bag.

ii. Ask the children to choose any four numbers between 0 and 31 and write them down. When they are ready, you pick out numbers from the bag, and call them out. The children check their numbers as you call them. The first child to match his or her four numbers wins a prize (e.g. a sweet), and becomes the caller for a repeat game.

## HOMEWORK

Ask the children to bring in two dice for the next lesson. Also ask them to bring in a range of junk materials. They will be making large beetles so ideally they will need bits of wool, coloured paper, buttons, and so on. Show your own materials as examples.

## ROUND UP

Review the song from Unit 2, Part 5 on the Class Cassette: *One, two, buckle my shoe.* Divide the class into two teams. Teams stand in two lines at the door facing each other. Team 1 sings the numbers, Team 2 sings and does the actions. Teams change roles and repeat the song. The class leaves at the end of the song.

*Tapescript* ○-6
*Unit 2, Part 5. Listen and join in.*
One, two, buckle my shoe. Three, four, knock at the door. Five, six, pick up sticks. Seven, eight, put them straight. Nine, ten, start again.

# Lesson 2
# Making a Beetle

## PREPARING YOUR LESSON

– Prepare very simple picture flash cards for parts of the beetle's body: *body, antennae, eyes, legs, tail.* Also draw a beetle (simple drawing) on the board.

– Bring in spare dice.

– Prepare lots of spare junk materials. Also provide large sheets of thin card or thick paper for the *giant beetles.*

– Make sure you have spare glue, crayons and scissors.

## WARM UP

Use the Action Game on the Class Cassette (Unit 3, Part 1). This is the second time the children have played this game, so follow Action Game Procedure 2 on page 18.

**Tapescript** 0 – 10
*Unit 3, Part 1. Listen and do the actions.*
Ready? Stand up please. Come here. Pick up a number. Say the number. Put the number down. Sit down.

## PRESENTING NEW LANGUAGE

• teaching the parts of the beetle's body
• active understanding of *this* and *these*
• encouraging the children to help each other and correct each other's errors
• group formation activity

Parts of the beetle's body. Use flash cards for body parts as teaching aids.

i.  Draw a quick picture of a beetle (as on page 6 of the Student's Book) on the board. Organise the class into a semi-circle. Refer to your drawing on the board so that the children have a context for the individual parts of the beetle. Give out the picture flash cards of the beetle's body to the children. You say the words as you give out the cards. Make one child responsible for one word. The children listen only.

ii.  You say the words. The children hold up the appropriate flash card. They don't speak.

iii.  The children exchange pictures. You say the words. The children holding the appropriate pictures hold them up. The remainder of the class draw the correct pictures in the air with their fingers.

iv.  Ask the children to put the flash cards on desk tops around the classroom. Organise the class into groups of three or four. Ask groups to stand around specific flash cards, touching the picture with their right hands. You then say the words. Groups touch the appropriate part of their own body when they hear their word. (They imagine *antennae* and *tail*.) They don't speak.

v.  Ask the children to move to a new flash card of their choice. You say the words. The children must *do an action* for the body part when they hear their word.

vi.  Ask the children to stand in a circle. You choose two flash cards: the *body* and *eyes*, for example. You walk around the group with these flash cards and teach them to various children. You encourage all the children to do the same with the pictures they are holding. Don't expect the children to repeat your complete sentences at this stage.
T–S1: *This is the body. These are the eyes.*
T–S2: *This is the body. These are the eyes.*
S1–S2: *(This is the) head.*
S2–S1: *(These are the) antennae.*
S3–S4: *(This is the) tail.*
You move into the background as the activity gathers momentum. Encourage the children to help and correct each other.

vii.  *Consolidation step:* You stop the activity. You name each of the parts of the beetle's body. The children listen only. The children then exchange flash cards and repeat the above activity.

## CHECK HOMEWORK

Check that the children have brought their dice and junk materials.

i.  The children display and sort the junk materials they have brought in onto a *materials table.* Organise the class layout for the next stage of the lesson, where the children will be working in groups of four or five. It is essential that each group has easy access to the materials table.

ii.  Check the results of throwing the dice 100 times. Draw a simple chart to show the results. Compare the results with the children's guesses from last lesson. Who guessed the best? Find out why.

## ACTIVITY

- making giant beetles
- group co-operation
- consolidation of vocabulary related to the beetle

Making a beetle.

a) Introduce the theme of the activity.

Organise the children into pairs. S1 sits behind S2. Play Unit 3, Part 2 on the Class Cassette. S1 draws the parts of the beetle (with his or her finger) on S2's back according to the instructions on the Cassette. Rewind the Cassette. The children change roles, then partners and repeat this activity.

*Tapescript* 11-27
*Unit 3, Part 2. Listen and draw the beetle.*
1. Draw one big head.
2. Draw two little eyes.
3. Draw two long antennae.
4. Draw one big, round body.
5. Draw six long legs.
6. Draw one little tail.

b) The children play *Beetle* (see Student's Book page 6). They play the game in pairs or threes.

*Rules*
The aim is to draw the complete beetle. Players throw a dice. To draw a part of the beetle's body a player must throw the correct number in the correct sequence. This sequence is shown on page 6.

i.   The children play the game once only.

ii.  Stop the activity. Introduce the *game* language. For example:
*my turn; my turn again; I got a three; fantastic; your turn; . . . six . . . finished!*

iii. Sit with one pair of children. The rest of the class observes. Play the game with the children. You cheat with the numbers you throw in order to focus on the *game* language.
T: *My turn . . . a one. Fantastic. The body. My turn again . . . a five. Your turn.*
S1 (+ T's help): *A two. Your turn.*
S2 (+ T's help): *A three. Your turn.*
T: *A two. Fantastic. The head. My turn again . . . a six. Your turn.*
S1 (+ T's help): *A one. Fantastic. The body. My turn again . . . etc.*

iv.  Sit with another pair of children and repeat your demonstration.

v.   The children change partners and play *Beetle* again. You go round the class and help with the language as necessary.

c) Making giant beetles.

i.   Divide the class into groups of four or five. Appoint a group leader who also acts as a *tidy monitor*. Explain and demonstrate the aims of the activity: to make a giant beetle. Explain that all the children must take part. The beetles must be the result of cutting and gluing, not merely drawing. Groups discuss the materials they need (in their mother tongue). Group leaders collect the materials from the materials table.

ii.  The children make their beetles. You go round and chat to the groups in English. Ask them questions, make comments, using lots of gestures to help explain your meaning. For example:
T: *Those are fantastic antennae. How long are they, do you think?*
S: *30 centimetres.*
T: *You're using buttons for the eyes . . . Everyone stop a moment. Look at these eyes. They're bright blue. Aren't they fantastic! Well done, this group . . . etc.*

*Note:* The main aim of this stage of the activity is for the children to make giant beetles. To do this, they need to co-operate as a group. This co-operation is, in itself, extremely important learning experience. At this stage of the course, however, the children do not have the language to discuss and chat in English. They will therefore chat in their mother tongue, probably introducing occasional English words. This is quite acceptable, since the other main purpose of this activity is to involve the children in the creation of a *language text*: once the beetles are completed, you will be using them as language texts.
As the course progresses, you encourage the children to ask for what they want in English, teaching the common classroom expressions and phrases as they occur naturally within an activity. For example: *Can I have a pencil?; I don't have any glue; Can I borrow your scissors?; Can I go to the toilet?; I've forgotten my eraser; Finished.* In addition, once the children have gained confidence they will, of their own accord, use more English while they are working in groups on practical activities.

iii. Stop the activity at least five minutes before the end of the lesson. Collect in and store the beetles.

iv.  Tidy up the classroom. Encourage the children to have the cleanest and tidiest work areas possible.

## REVIEW

*994·000*

Review the song from Unit 2, Part 5 on the Class Cassette: *One, two, buckle my shoe.*

## HOMEWORK

Ask the children to find and bring in pictures of real beetles, or books containing pictures of real beetles.

## ROUND UP

- reviewing numbers and colours
- group formation activity
- friendship and trust activity

Play a story game using *numbers* and *colours* as the key words.

i.   Organise the class into two teams. The teams line up in front of the board, about one metre between the two lines. The children turn to face each other and form pairs with the children facing them.

ii.  Pairs join hands and raise their arms, thus forming a sort of archway or tunnel.

iii. Assign each pair (S1 from Team 1 and S1 from Team 2) of children a number: *1–4*, or a colour: *brown, green, blue, red*. Make up a simple story which contains these numbers and colours. When the children hear their number or colour, they must race their partner under the arch of arms, to the back of the line, then back to their places. Team mates shout: *Come on, come on*, as encouragement. The first child back scores a team point.

### Example Story Script

*One day last week, I went shopping with my mum and dad. I had to buy a **red** sweater . . . and **three** pairs . . . of **blue** socks for school. We waited at the bus stop for a number **two** bus. It was a lovely day. The sky was **blue** and there were **two**, . . . **red** and **brown** butterflies . . . etc.*

*Note:* You can use this story game technique to review other vocabulary at any time during the course.

# Lesson 3
# Follow Up Activities

## PREPARING YOUR LESSON

– Prepare your own Unit 3 Workpage (Student's Book page 7) for demonstration purposes.

– Bring in the children's *giant beetles*.

## WARM UP

- group formation
- consolidating *parts of the body* vocabulary

Play the Action Game on the Class Cassette (Unit 3, Part 2).

*Tapescript*  11-27          *draw & label & colour*
*Unit 3, Part 2. Listen and draw the beetle.*
1. Draw one big head.
2. Draw two little eyes.
3. Draw two long antennae.
4. Draw one big, round body.
5. Draw six long legs.
6. Draw one little tail.

Although this is only the second time the children have played this game, follow (the adapted) Action Game Procedure 3 below:

i.   The children sit in pairs. S1 sits behind S2. You play/say the complete script. S1s draw the beetle on their partners' backs (no speaking). You watch the children.

ii.  Pairs change roles. S1 sits in front of S2. You play/say (softly) the Action Game script. S1 repeats with (not after) you or the Cassette. S2 draws (with his or her finger) the parts of the beetle on S1's back according to S1's instructions. Don't correct errors at this stage.

iii. The children change roles and give their own instructions. You go round the class helping if necessary. Whenever feasible say the complete script while the children are listening. Then let them try. Encourage student-to-student correction rather than allowing the children merely to repeat line by line after you.

## CHECK HOMEWORK

i.   Ask the children to show you their pictures and picture books of real beetles.

ii. Organise the class into groups of four. The children share their 'beetle' information. Go round and chat to the children, encouraging them, where feasible, to use English to describe the beetles in the pictures.

## REVIEW AND LANGUAGE PRACTICE

- active understanding of *throwing a dice* language
- using the expressions:
  *What number did you get?*
  *What number did you get this time?*
- team game

Play *Team beetle.*

i. Divide the class into two teams. S1 from each team comes to the board, and takes turns to speak. Use Unit 3, Part 3 on the Class Cassette. You play the Cassette. Pause the Cassette after each question, rewind and play the question again, encouraging S1 to ask the questions with the Cassette. S2 from each team throws a dice and answers S1's question. S1 draws parts of the beetle if the number is appropriate (refer to page 6: 1 = body, 2 = head, etc.). The children take turns at the board, and at throwing the dice.

*Tapescript* 27-38
*Unit 3, Part 3. Throw a dice. Listen and say what number you throw each time.*
Pair work
1. Throw the dice. What number did you get?
2. Throw the dice again. What number did you get this time?
3. Throw the dice again. What number did you get this time?

Don't correct errors while the children are speaking. If there are errors, when one child has finished, and before asking a new student to speak, you take a turn and give the class another chance to listen to a correct version.

ii. Repeat the game, and the game procedure. This time use Unit 3, Part 4 on the Class Cassette.

*Tapescript* 38-46
Pair work *Unit 3, Part 4. Throw a dice. Listen and answer yes or no.*
1. Throw the dice. Did you get a six?
2. Throw the dice again. Did you get a four?
3. Throw the dice again. Did you get a five?

Encourage the children to ask similar questions of their own. For example:
S1: *Throw the dice again. Did you get a two?*
S2: *No. A four.*
S1: *Throw the dice again. Did you get a two this time?*
S2: *No. A three . . . etc.*

## LANGUAGE PRACTICE

- describing their beetles (use of *this is / these are; has [got]*)
- consolidation of the language learned in this Unit

Describing the beetles.

i. Give out the beetles that were completed last lesson. Comment on each one. Ask the class general questions about colour, size, shape and number.

ii. You give an example. Point to a beetle as you speak:
T: *This is my beetle. It's got a big, round head. It's got two red eyes. It's got two long antennae, a big round body. It's got six little legs and a tiny, curly tail.*

iii. You repeat your description, leaving out key words. The class says the missing words.
T: *This is my . . .*
Ss: *Beetle.*
T: *It's got a big . . .*
Ss: *Round head . . . etc.*

iv. S1 comes to the front of the class. He or she points to parts of the beetle. The class describes them. Repeat this activity with a new S1.

v. Organise the children into groups of three or four. The children take turns to describe their beetles to their group. You go round and help with the language. Whenever feasible say a complete description while the children are listening. Then let them try. Encourage student-to-student correction rather than allowing the children merely to repeat line by line after you.

vi. Choose and encourage children to talk about their beetles to the rest of the class. Allow errors. Don't correct the children as they speak. Encourage all attempts. If needed, when a child has finished, repeat your example. Get other children to try.

## WORKPAGE

- recording work done in this Unit
- reviewing and consolidating

Complete the Workpage, Student's Book page 7. Use Unit 3, Parts A, B and C on the Home Cassette.

i. Demonstrate how to do Part A.

*Tapescript* 11-27
*Unit 3, Part A. Listen, and draw. Colour your drawing. Write in the missing words.*
1. Draw one big head.
2. Draw two little eyes.
3. Draw two long antennae.
4. Draw one big, round body.
5. Draw six long legs.
6. Draw one little tail.

When the children understand what to do, play the Cassette again. The children draw the beetle in their books.

ii. Demonstrate how to do Parts B and C. Show your own Workpage. When the children understand what to do, organise the class into pairs. Each pair has a dice. You play the Cassette. Pause the Cassette after each question, rewind and play the question again, encouraging S1 in each pair to ask the questions with the Cassette. S2 throws the dice and answers. The children change roles, then partners and repeat the activity. You go round the class helping where necessary.

*Tapescript* 27-38
*Unit 3, Part B. Throw a dice. Listen. Draw the number you throw each time.*
1. Throw the dice. What number did you get?
2. Throw the dice again. What number did you get this time?
3. Throw the dice again. What number did you get this time?

38-46
*Unit 3, Part C. Throw a dice. Listen. Write yes or no.*
1. Throw the dice. Did you get a six?
2. Throw the dice again. Did you get a four?
3. Throw the dice again. Did you get a five?

iii. Finally, ask the children to throw a dice and record their answers on page 7 of their *early bird* books.

## HOMEWORK

- encouraging the children to observe insects in their natural habitat
- finding out how many main body parts a real beetle has

Ask the children to observe (but not to collect or disturb) real beetles (or other mini-beasts). Ask them to draw one beetle and bring the drawing to the next lesson. How many body parts does a real beetle have? Ask the children to guess and to find out. Encourage the children to ask their parents to sign their completed Workpage.

## ROUND UP

Teach *Head, body, legs and tail* using Unit 3, Part 5 on the Class Cassette. Encourage the children to use gestures as they sing.

*Tapescript* 46-64    Give out photocopies
*Unit 3, Part 5. Listen and join in.*
Head, body, legs and tail. Legs and tail.
Head, body, legs and tail. Legs and tail.
And eyes and ears and nose and nail.
Head, body, legs and tail. Legs and tail.

## EVALUATION

- evaluating informally what the children have learned

In terms of evaluation of this Unit, the following table can be used as a guide. You may photocopy and include it in your school record book. For simplicity, tick a column if you are satisfied with a child's performance; leave it blank if you are not happy. *Note:* The table is a guide, and a record to refer back to. It is not intended as a grade list.

| Name | Activity completed | Can give the PR instructions for this Unit | Can understand your questions about numbers and beetles | Can give true responses | Can communicate information about the beetle |
|------|------|------|------|------|------|
|  |  |  |  |  |  |
|  |  |  |  |  |  |
|  |  |  |  |  |  |
|  |  |  |  |  |  |

# Unit 4    Picture Dictionary Work

## INTRODUCTION

This is the first Dictionary Unit in the course. The aims are as follows:

- introducing the children to the sorting and filing of items according to a dictionary category or heading;

- encouraging the children to start their own, independent Picture Dictionary, using the headings and items from *early bird* as a central core;

- consolidating awareness of an alphabetical filing system;

- introducing spelling in English;

- reviewing and previewing vocabulary.

## Content and Format of Dictionary Activity Pages

- The Dictionary Activity Pages review and preview the key vocabulary from the course. They are introduced at regular intervals: Units 4, 8 and 11 in *early bird 1*.

- The vocabulary is presented in picture form, with the written words printed under each picture. The children cut up the page, sort and classify this vocabulary by *category*, for example: *colours, family, food and drink*. Once classified, the children glue the items onto the appropriate page, and under the appropriate category, in their *early bird* book. The Dictionary Activity Pages are therefore printed in the *Activity Cut-Outs* section at the back of the *early bird* Student's Book.

- Since the children will also file these vocabulary items in their own, independent Picture Dictionary, the Dictionary Activity Pages are printed in duplicate. The children use the items from the second copy for their independent Dictionary. The printed words are omitted from the second copy.

- 32 *picture headings*, printed in alphabetical order on page 45 of the *early bird* Student's Book, act as a picture index for the children's independent Picture Dictionary. A duplicate of these headings is printed on page 47. The children cut up page 47 and glue each heading at the top of its own blank page in their new Picture Dictionaries.

## Preparing for the first Dictionary Lesson (Unit 4)

i. Before your first Dictionary Lesson, prepare your own Picture Dictionary in advance. Use a blank, A4 size, loose leaf book or file (so that new pages can be inserted when necessary), with a strong, plain cover, containing about 25 blank sheets of paper (50 pages).

ii. Decorate the cover with a Picture Dictionary or *early bird* design of your choice.

iii. Turn to page 45 of the *early bird* Student's Book. Remove this sheet and glue or file it at the front of your blank Picture Dictionary. This creates a picture index for your new Dictionary, consisting of 32 picture headings.

iv. Turn to page 47 of the *early bird* Student's Book. Cut up this sheet, note the alphabetical order, and glue each heading at the top of its own blank page. You now have 32 headed pages, filed in alphabetical order. The picture vocabulary from *early bird* will be filed on these pages.

v. Turn to page 8 of the *early bird* Student's Book. Note that this page contains four headings: *colours, food and drink, numbers, action*. Each heading has a clearly defined area on the page.

vi. Turn to page 27. Note that the main vocabulary content is printed on this page. The children will cut out, sort and classify these items, finally gluing them under the appropriate headings on page 8. For demonstration purposes, cut up your page 27. Glue the items onto page 8 under their appropriate headings.

vii. Turn to page 29. This is a duplicate of page 27. However, the printed words have been omitted. The items on this page will be filed in the independent Picture Dictionaries that the children create themselves. For demonstration purposes, cut out the items on your own page 29. File the items under their appropriate headings in your new Picture Dictionary.

*Note:* The *action* heading is printed on pages 27 and 29, not on pages 45 and 47. Since this is a different kind of category from the rest of the headings, it is practical to file it, as a page heading, at the back of the Picture Dictionary. Consequently, *action pictures* from page 29 should also be filed under the *action* heading at the back of the Picture Dictionary.

viii. Prepare flash cards for the four headings: *colours, food and drink, numbers, action.* One practical method is to make enlarged photocopies for each heading. Ask the children to colour them as an additional *preview* activity.

ix. Make simple flash cards for the new items on page 27.

## What you ask the children to prepare

i. Ask the children to prepare their own Picture Dictionaries in advance. Suggest they use an A4 size, loose leaf file or book (so that new pages can be inserted when necessary), with a strong plain cover, containing about 25 blank sheets of paper (50 pages).

ii. Ask them to decorate the cover with a Picture Dictionary or *early bird* design of their choice. Show your Dictionary as an example.

*Note:* The children invest a considerable amount of time on their Picture Dictionaries throughout the *early bird* course. They themselves decide where items should be filed. They create their own new headings, and search out new items to file. In other words, the children are active and involved partners in the building of their own personal Picture Dictionaries.

Table 1 (below) summarises the content of the Unit. Table 2 gives an outline of the key teaching steps.

**Table 1**

| The Children's Experience of Language Input across the Curriculum | | | Language Output from the Children in an Activity-Based Context | |
| --- | --- | --- | --- | --- |
| Activities and topics | Teacher's questions, instructions, and comments about: | Physical Response Activities | Vocabulary | Expressions and structures |
| Picture Dictionary | sorting and classifying words; displaying cut-outs | hold up point to cut out glue in count put under | ketchup hamburger french fries hot dog pizza *colours* *food* *numbers* | I do/don't here/there<br><br>Maria's, Toni's . . . (possessive s)<br><br>Who has . . . ? Who is . . . ? |

**Table 2**

| Lesson 1<br>Preparation Activities | Lesson 2<br>Main Activity:<br>Picture Dictionary Work | Lesson 3<br>Follow Up Activities |
|---|---|---|
| Warm Up: play *Twister* with colours | Warm Up: play *What colour changed position?* | Warm Up: Action Game: use Class Cassette Unit 4, Part 3 (follow Procedure 3) |
| Check Homework: feedback on the mini-beast observation results; colour in *star 3* | Check Homework: check the envelopes are glued in and decorated | Check Homework: get the children started on their own Picture Dictionaries |
| Presenting New Language: fast food items; recognition of spellings | Main Activity: the children sort and file the items from Student's Book page 27 under the headings on page 8; tell the children what to prepare for their Picture Dictionaries | Unit 4 Workpage (Student's Book page 9): use Home Cassette, Unit 4, Parts B and C |
| Action Game: use the script from Class Cassette Unit 1, Part 2 (follow Procedure 1) | Review: Action Game: use the script from Unit 1, Part 2 (follow Procedure 3); asking and answering measurement questions | Review: Unit 1 – asking and answering measurements questions – use Class Cassette Unit 1, Part 4 |
| Review and Language Practice: Unit 1 – counting instructions | Language Practice: classroom instructions | Game or Song: free choice |
| Homework: *bits and pieces* envelope | Homework: bring in a blank book for own Picture Dictionary | Homework: Picture Dictionary work |
| Round Up: the children sing: *Head, body, legs and tail* – use Class Cassette Unit 3, Part 5 | Round Up: play *Scissors, stone, paper* | Round Up: play story game with *food* and *colours* |

*Note:* The review Unit is Unit 1.

# Lesson 1
# Preparation Activities

## PREPARING YOUR LESSON

– Prepare picture flash cards for vocabulary items on Activity Page 8 of the Student's Book. One method is to make enlarged photocopies of the items and then ask the children to colour them in. Alternatively, ask the children to draw large copies for you in advance.

– Prepare *word* flash cards for each of the items.

– Glue a *bits and pieces* envelope onto the front inside cover of your own *early bird* book for demonstration purposes.

– Complete your own Activity Page and Workpage for Unit 3.

– Bring in your own drawing of a real beetle or mini-beast. Note that all insects have six legs and three main body parts (head, neck and body). Non-insects have more or fewer legs and body segments.

## WARM UP

Play *Twister* with the colours. Use your colour flash cards, and ask the children to colour sheets of paper to make additional flash cards.

### Rules
The children receive instructions to touch the colours with various parts of their body. For example:

T: *Touch yellow with your left hand. Now, touch green with your right elbow. Now, touch blue with your left knee. OK, let go of yellow and touch pink with your left hand . . . etc.*

The children must keep touching all the colours until instructed otherwise. Those who fall over or fail to touch, are out of the game or lose a team point.

i. Organise the class into groups of five. Ask groups to make simple flash cards for the colours by colouring in pieces of paper. In this way, each group should produce five or six colours.

ii. Ask the groups to pick up their colours and put them on desk tops or the floor. Make sure that the colours are reasonably close together for the game.

iii. Demonstrate how to play with S1 and S2. Use lots of gestures to explain the parts of the body you want the children to use.

iv. Play the game.

v. Develop the activity: let S1 take your role. S1 gives the *Twister* instructions to the group. Don't correct S1 while he or she is speaking. If there are errors, when a child has finished, and before asking a new student to be the teacher, you have another turn and give the class an additional chance to listen to a correct version.
T: *Marie. Your turn. You give the instructions.*
S: *Put your left hand on yellow. Put your left foot on green . . . etc.*
T: *My turn again. Put your nose on green . . . etc.*

## CHECK HOMEWORK

• encouraging the children to evaluate their own work and other children's work
• consolidating language from Unit 3
• talking about the results of observing real beetles or mini-beasts

a) Ask the children to show their pictures, then talk about the beetles and mini-beasts they have drawn for homework.

i. You give the example. Point to a beetle as you speak.
T: *This is my beetle. It has two long antennae, six legs, three body parts – head, neck and body. It's brown. It has two big eyes.*

ii. You repeat your description, leaving out key words. The class says the missing words.
T: *This is my . . .*
Ss: *Beetle.*
T: *It has two . . .*
Ss: *Long antennae . . . etc.*

iii. S1 comes to the front of the class. S1 holds up his or her drawing and points to parts of the beetle. The class describes them. Repeat this activity with a new S1.

iv. Organise the children into groups of three or four. The children take turns to describe their beetles to their group. You go round and help with the language. Whenever feasible say a complete description while the children are listening. Then let them try. Encourage student-to-student correction rather than allowing the children merely to repeat line by line after you.

v. Choose and encourage children to talk about their beetles and mini-beasts to the rest of the class. Allow errors. Don't correct the children as they speak. Encourage all attempts. If needed, when a child has finished, repeat your own description. Get other children to try.

b) <u>Grading Unit 3.</u>

i. Show your completed pages for Unit 3. As for previous Units, ask the children what colour (grade) you deserve for your work. Turn to the *star chart* on the inside back cover of the book. Abide by the class decision on your grade, and colour in *star 3* on the star chart.

ii. Ask the children to work in pairs. The children colour in their partner's *star* for this Unit. If there is any dispute, ask another child to be the final judge of grade.

iii. Check that parents have signed their children's Workpage.

## PRESENTING NEW LANGUAGE

• reviewing vocabulary
• introducing spelling of the vocabulary from this Unit
• teaching *How do you spell . . . ?*

a) Review the vocabulary on page 27 of the *early bird* Student's Book. Use picture flash cards or real items as teaching aids.

i. <u>Show and name the items or flash cards.</u> The children watch and listen only.
T: *This is a hamburger. These are french fries . . . etc.*

ii. Ask the children to *pick up and give* items to the other children.
T: *Rikki. Pick up the ketchup. Give it to Yoshiko . . . etc.*

iii. Give *eat* or *play* instructions. The children pick up and *eat* the food items.
T: *Mari, pick up the hamburger. Open your mouth. Wider. Bite the hamburger. Yum.*

iv. Ask the children to identify the items they are holding. Use gestures to help explain your meaning.
T: *Who has the pizza? Me or you?*
S: *Me.*
T: *Elsie, who has the colour blue?*
S: *Toni . . . etc.*

v. Ask the children to stand in a circle. You choose one flash card. You walk around the group with this flash card and teach it to various children. You encourage all the children to do the same with the flash cards they are holding. Move into the background as this activity gathers momentum. Encourage the children to help and correct each other.

vi. *Consolidation step:* You stop the activity. You say each of the words. The children listen only. The children then exchange flash cards and repeat the above activity.

b) Focus on spelling[1].
Organise the class into two teams. The teams stand or sit in a large semi-circle. Collect in all the picture flash cards (and items) and lay them face down on the floor or desks. Display the *word* flash cards, word upwards, on the floor or desks. The children from each team take turns to compete against each other in a variety of mini-challenges. For example:

i. You name a vocabulary item. The first <u>child</u> to <u>touch the word</u> for that item scores a team point – if he or she can then <u>match the spelling</u> to the real item or picture of the item.

ii. You <u>start to spell a word.</u> The first <u>child</u> to <u>guess the word</u> you are spelling scores a team point.

iii. You ask the two competing children to close their eyes. Ask them how to spell one word each. Correct spelling scores a point.
T: *How do you spell yellow? . . . etc.*

iv. Ask S1 to take your role. He or she asks the spelling questions. Don't correct while S1 is speaking. If there are errors, when a child has finished, and before asking a new student to be the teacher, you have another turn. In this way you give the class another chance to listen to a correct example.

v. Finally, organise the children into pairs. The children turn to page 27. S1 asks a spelling. S2 spells the word without looking at the page:
S1: *How do you spell yellow?*
S2: *y . . . e . . . l . . . l . . . o . . . w . . . etc.*

## ACTION GAME

Use an extract from the script of Unit 1, Part 2 on the Class Cassette. Follow Action Game Procedure 1 on page 15.

*Tapescript*
*Unit 1, Part 2. Listen and do the actions.*
Reach up with your arms. Higher. Higher. Relax.
Now stretch your arms out. Wider. Wider. Relax.
Now. Right foot. Stand on your right foot, and hop.
1 . . . 2 . . . 3 . . . hop. Left foot. Stand on your left foot. 1 . . . 2 . . . 3 . . . hop.

[1] This spelling activity may be inappropriate for younger children, in which case omit it for the time being.

## REVIEW AND LANGUAGE PRACTICE

- reviewing selected content from Unit 1
- *counting* and *counting* instructions in English
- using *from* and *to*

i.  Demonstrate the activity: organise the children into groups of four or five. Use Unit 4, Part 1 on the Class Cassette. You play the Cassette. Choose groups to count the correct numbers.

    *Tapescript*
    *Unit 4, Part 1. Listen and count the right numbers.*
    1. Count to 10.
    2. Count to 20.
    3. Count from 8 to 12.
    4. Count from 6 to 15.

ii. Add counting instructions of your own.

iii. Ask S1 to give the *counting* instructions. If there are errors, when a child has finished, and before asking a new student to be the teacher, you have another turn in order to give the class another chance to listen to a correct example.
    T: *Who wants to be teacher? Hands up . . . Toni, you try.*
    S: *Count (from) 3 to 12 . . . etc.*
    T: *My turn again. Count from 5 to 15 . . . etc.*

iv. Pairwork. S1 of each pair gives the counting instructions. S2 counts. You go round the class and help with the language if needed. As before, discourage the children from merely repeating after you. Give the children complete examples to listen to, leave the group, and allow them time to practise. Return later to check on results.

## HOMEWORK

Ask the children to find a suitable *bits and pieces* envelope. They glue this envelope onto the inside cover of their book, and decorate it. Demonstrate how to do this. Show your own envelope, glued onto the inside cover.

## ROUND UP

Review the song from Unit 3, Part 5 on the Class Cassette: *Head, body, legs and tail.*

# Lesson 2
# Picture Dictionary Work

## PREPARING THE LESSON

– Prepare large simple flash cards for the headings on page 8 of the Student's Book: *food and drink, numbers, colours, action.* One method is to make enlarged photocopies of the headings, and glue them onto thin card.

– Bring in the flash cards for the vocabulary items that you used last lesson.

– Bring in spare *bits and pieces* envelopes.

– Read the Introduction section for this Unit. Prepare your independent *early bird* Picture Dictionary so you can show the children how to make theirs.

## WARM UP

- focusing attention on visual sequence
- consolidating *colours* vocabulary

Play *What colour changed position?* Use flash cards of the colours as teaching aids.

i.  Organise the class into a large semi-circle. Choose S1 and Group 1. S1 closes eyes. Group 1 displays the colour flash cards in an order of their choice. S1 opens eyes and looks at the colours for five seconds, then closes eyes again.

ii. The group exchanges the positions of two colours. S1 opens eyes, and tries to identify the change.

iii. Repeat the activity with a new S1 and a new group.

## CHECK HOMEWORK

Get the children to show you their new *bits and pieces* envelopes. Have spare envelopes available for any children who have forgotten theirs.

## ACTIVITY

Dictionary work with the items on page 27 of the *early bird* book.

a)  Teach the four Picture Dictionary Headings on page 8.

    i.  Organise the class into a large semi-circle.

    ii. You show and name each *heading* flash card. The children watch and listen only.
        T: *This is the food and drink heading, here. This is the numbers heading, here . . . etc.*

iii. Display the headings on the board or wall. Ask the children to point to the various headings. The children don't speak at this stage.
T: *Point to the numbers heading. Now point to . . . etc.*

iv. Ask the children to stand under the headings.
T: *Jeanne, stand under the colours heading. Marianne, stand under the food and drink heading . . . etc.*

v. Ask the children to identify the headings:
T: *Who's standing under the food and drink heading? Hands up. What heading is Maria standing under, Pepi?*
S: *Numbers . . . etc.*

b) Cutting out the items.

i. Organise the class into groups of three or four. The children sit in their groups. Choose a *tidy monitor* for each group.

ii. Check that all groups have access to a pair of scissors.

iii. Ask the children to turn to pages 27 and 29 of their *early bird* books. Point out the differences between pages 27 and 29.

iv. Give instructions to cut out items from page 27.
T: *Does everybody have a pair of scissors? Everyone hold up your scissors. Now, cut out the french fries. Only the french fries . . . What picture are we going to cut out next? Yellow or pink or the hot dog?*
S: *Hot dog.*
T: *Hands up if you think we're going to cut out the hot dog next. . . Well you're right. We're going to cut out the hot dog. Everybody cut out the hot dog . . . etc.*

v. Give these types of instructions for four items, then ask the children to continue cutting out the rest of the items by themselves.

vi. Ask the children to cut up page 29. They put these items in their *bits and pieces* envelopes. When they have finished, organise the class into a semi-circle.

c) Sorting and filing the items from page 27 onto page 8 of the *early bird* book.

i. Put your flash cards of the headings on the board.

ii. Show the flash cards for the vocabulary items. Ask the children to put the flash cards of the vocabulary items under the correct headings.
T: *What's this, Miki?*
S: *A hamburger.*
T: *Where does the hamburger go? Which*

*heading? Colours? Food and drink? Where does it go? Show me.*
S: *Here . . . etc.*

iii. The children put several of the items under the correct headings. Get consensus opinion from the class for each item.

iv. The class work in their groups and sort all their items from page 27 under the headings printed on page 8. You go round and ask questions about the vocabulary and the classification of the items.
T: *What's this colour, Freddie?*
S: *Yellow.*
T: *Which heading does it go under?*
S: *Colours . . . etc.*

d) Picture Dictionary Work. As discussed in the Introduction to this Unit, in order to develop this dictionary skills activity into a Picture Dictionary, each child must have his or her own blank book in which to file all the vocabulary items.

i. Show your own Picture Dictionary. Point out that it should be A4 size, have a loose leaf format, and a strong cover.

ii. Ask the children to turn to the two copies of the *picture headings* on pages 45 and 47 of their *early bird* books.

iii. Show how page 45 is used as a *picture index* for the Dictionary.

iv. Show how the headings on page 47 are cut up and used to create pages in the Dictionary, demonstrating how you have created the first four pages of your own Picture Dictionary: *alphabet, animals, art and craft, body.*

v. For homework, ask the children to bring in a suitable blank book for their Picture Dictionaries for the next lesson. Ask them to design and decorate the covers of their Dictionaries. (Give the children two homeworks to complete this task.)

## REVIEW

• reviewing the Workpage from Unit 1

a) Use an extract from the script of Unit 1, Part 2 on the Class Cassette. Follow Action Game Procedure 3 on page 23.

*Tapescript*
*Unit 1, Part 2. Listen and do the actions.*
Reach up with your arms. Higher. Higher. Relax. Now stretch your arms out. Wider. Wider. Relax. Now. Right foot. Stand on your right foot, and hop. 1 . . . 2 . . . 3 . . . hop. Left foot. Stand on your left foot. 1 . . . 2 . . . 3 . . . hop.

Unit 4

b) Encourage the children to ask each other questions about their personal measurements.

   i. Organise the children into a semi-circle. Ask them to turn to page 3 of their *early bird* books. Ask them *measurements* questions. They look at the information they have recorded and give you true answers.

   ii. Organise the children into groups of three or four. Use Unit 1, Part 3 on the Class Cassette.

   iii. Choose a leader for each group. Play the Cassette. Pause the Cassette after each question, rewind and play the question again, encouraging the leaders to ask the questions with the Cassette. Group members answer. Don't correct errors at this stage.

*Tapescript*
*Unit 1, Part 3. Listen and give true answers.*
1. How old are you?
2. How tall are you?
3. How much do you weigh?
4. How long is your foot?

   iv. Change leaders. Repeat the activity, without the Cassette. You go round the class and help with the language if needed. As before, don't encourage the children merely to repeat after you. Give the children complete examples to listen to, leave the group, and allow them time to practise. Return later to check on results.

## LANGUAGE PRACTICE

- practising classroom instructions

i. Organise the class into pairs. The children take out their dictionary items from their *bits and pieces* envelopes.

ii. Play Unit 4, Part 2 on the Class Cassette. The children find and hold up the correct items.

*Tapescript*
*Unit 4, Part 2. Listen, pick up the right picture. Hold it up.*
1. Hold up the hot dog, please.
2. Hold up the hamburger, please.
3. Hold up the ketchup, please.
4. Hold up the french fries, please.
5. Hold up something blue.
6. Hold up something pink.
7. Hold up something green.
8. Hold up something yellow.
9. Hold up something red.
10. Hold up the pizza.

iii. Choose S1. Replay the Cassette. S1 gives the instructions with the Cassette. The class holds up the correct pictures.

iv. Change S1. Repeat the activity without the Cassette.

v. Pairwork. Repeat the activity without the Cassette. You go round the class and help with the language if needed. As before, don't encourage the children merely to repeat after you. Give the children complete examples to listen to, leave the group, and allow them time to practise. Return later to check on results.

vi. The children return their items to the *bits and pieces* envelope at the end of the activity.

## HOMEWORK

i. Ask the children to bring in a suitable blank book for their Picture Dictionaries for the next lesson, and to decorate the cover with their own Dictionary design.

ii. Ask the children to finish off any incomplete cutting or gluing.

## ROUND UP

Play *Scissors, stone, paper.* This is a traditional game children play when they want to select a partner, or a leader.

*Rules*
The children play the game in pairs to the chant of: *Scissors, stone, paper.*
The children show their choice with their right hands:

- *scissors* is shown with *two open fingers;*
- *stone* is shown with a *closed fist;*
- *paper* is shown with an *open hand.*

The children show their choice at the same time. The winner is decided according to the following rules:

- *scissors cut paper;*
- *stone blunts scissors;*
- *paper wraps stone.*

Winners play each other until a class winner emerges. The winner is allowed to leave the class first. Play the game twice more, then allow all the children to leave the class.

# Lesson 3
# Follow Up Activities

## PREPARING YOUR LESSON

– Prepare your Workpage (Student's Book page 9) for demonstration purposes.

– Glue the items from page 29 into your Picture Dictionary.

## WARM UP

• reviewing the initial Action Game from Unit 1

Use the Action Game on the Class Cassette (Unit 4, Part 3). Follow Action Game Procedure 3.

*Tapescript*
*Unit 4, Part 3. Listen and do the actions.*
Ready? Put your hand up. Put your hand down. Stand up. Come here. Go over there. Sit down. Thank you.

## CHECK HOMEWORK

• getting the children started on their Picture Dictionaries

i.  Organise the children into groups of four. Make sure that each group has access to pairs of scissors.

ii. Ask the children to turn to the *picture headings* on page 45 of their *early bird* books. They remove this sheet and glue or file it at the front of their blank Picture Dictionaries. They now have a *picture index* for their new Picture Dictionary, consisting of 32 picture headings.

iii. Ask the children to turn to the picture headings on page 47 of their *early bird* books. Ask them to cut out the *alphabet* heading. Show them where to glue it. Repeat for the next six headings.

iv. At this stage, check that the children understand:

– that each heading is filed in alphabetical order;

– that each heading goes onto a separate page;

– that the Picture Dictionary will be used throughout the course.

v.  Ask the children to turn to their new *colours* page in their Picture Dictionaries. Ask them to file the *colours* cut-outs from the *bits and pieces* envelope onto this page. Ask the children to write (copy) the *spellings* of the colours under the pictures.

vi. Ask the children to finish off gluing each heading at the top of its own blank page at home. Also ask them to file the remaining items from page 29 into their new Picture Dictionaries, and write in the *spellings*.

## WORKPAGE

• recording work done in this Unit
• reviewing and consolidating

Complete the Workpage, Student's Book page 9. Use Unit 4, Parts B and C on the Home Cassette.

i.  Demonstrate how to do Part A. The children must complete the missing information, and colour in where appropriate. Do the first two examples in class, and assign the remainder for homework.

ii. Demonstrate how to do Part B. Use Unit 4, Part B on the Home Cassette.
– Show your own page 9.
– When the children understand what to do, organise the class into pairs.
– You play the Cassette. Pause the Cassette after each instruction, rewind and play the instruction again, encouraging S1 in each pair to speak with the Cassette. S2 counts the appropriate numbers.
– The children change roles, then partners and repeat the activity. You go round the class helping where necessary. Finally, the children circle the correct numbers in each example.

*Tapescript*
*Unit 4, Part B. Listen. Count the right numbers.*
*Circle the numbers you've counted.*
1. Count to 10.
2. Count to 20.
3. Count from 8 to 12.
4. Count from 6 to 15.

iii. Review how to do Part C, the *Teach your parents* activity at home[2]. Use Unit 4, Part C on the Home Cassette. Follow a similar procedure to the one used in Unit 2. Do a role play for the *Teach your parents* situation. Choose two children. S1 is the parent. S2 is him- or herself:
– Ask S2 to give the class a short practical demonstration on how to use the cassette player. Encourage him or her to use the expression *like this* as he or she explains.

---

[2]   This activity may be too difficult for younger children. With a younger class, you will need to do a higher percentage of the Workpage activities in class time.

- Role play: S2 plays the Cassette and demonstrates the actions on the Cassette. S1 (the parent) watches and listens.
- S2 plays the Cassette again and does the actions with S1 (the parent).
- S2 gives the instructions with the Cassette. S1 (the parent) does the actions.

*Tapescript*
*Unit 4, Part C. Listen. Teach your parents.*
Ready? Put your hand up. Put your hand down. Stand up. Come here. Go over there. Sit down. Thank you.

## REVIEW

i. Organise the children into a semi-circle. Ask them to turn to page 3 of their *early bird* books. Ask them *measurements* questions. They look at the information they have recorded and give you true answers.

ii. Organise the children into groups of three or four. Use Unit 1, Part 4 on the Class Cassette.

iii. Choose a leader for each group. Play the Cassette. Pause the Cassette after each question, rewind and play the question again, encouraging the leaders to ask the questions with the Cassette. Group members answer. Don't correct errors at this stage.

*Tapescript*
*Unit 1, Part 4. Listen and give true answers*
1. How high can you reach?
2. How far can you stretch?
3. How high can you jump?
4. How far can you hop?

iv. Change leaders. Repeat the activity without the Cassette.

## GAME OR SONG

Free choice. Ask the children if they want to play a game, or sing. Suggest *Bingo* (with the items on page 27), or one of the three songs learnt so far.

## HOMEWORK

i. Ask the children to cut out and glue the remaining headings into their Picture Dictionaries. Confirm the alphabetical sequence of the activity.

ii. Ask the children to glue the remaining items from page 29 (now kept in their *bits and pieces* envelopes) into their Picture Dictionaries under the appropriate headings.

iii. Ask the children to draw (or find a cut-out from a magazine) one additional item for their *numbers, colours, food and drink* pages.

iv. Encourage the children to ask their parents to sign their completed Workpage.

## ROUND UP

Play a story game. Use a similar procedure to the story game stage of Unit 3, Lesson 2. Assign *food* and *colours* as the key words.

*Example Story Script*
*I love juicy **hamburgers** . . . with lots and lots of **red ketchup** . . . One day I went into a **hamburger** . . . store. I was starving. The smell of **french fries** . . . was fantastic. Suddenly I saw my friend, Annie. She was wearing a **pink** . . . dress, and eating a . . . etc.*

## EVALUATION

In terms of evaluation of this Unit, the following table can be used as a guide. You may photocopy and include it in your school record book. For simplicity, tick a column if you are satisfied with a child's performance; leave it blank if you are not happy. *Note:* The table is a guide, and a record to refer back to. It is not intended as a grade list.

| Name | Has sorted and classified items successfully | Has started own Picture Dictionary | Can understand your questions about dictionary items | Can give true responses | Can communicate information about own Dictionary pages |
|---|---|---|---|---|---|
| | | | | | |
| | | | | | |
| | | | | | |

# Unit 5    Making a Snapdragon

## INTRODUCTION

This Unit reviews vocabulary items from previous Units.

– The main activity is making a Snapdragon and playing *Snapdragon*.

– Playing *Snapdragon* requires children to spell and use the alphabet. The children only need to learn the spelling of the four colours on the Snapdragon as discrete items, and not use the alphabet system as a whole.

Through the practical activities in Unit 5, the children will:

– practise cutting and folding accurately;

– spell the vocabulary on the Snapdragon;

– give a variety of simple instructions in English;

– use gestures and language to explain how they made their Snapdragon.

Table 1 (below) summarises the content of the Unit. Table 2 gives an outline of the key teaching steps.

## Table 1

| The Children's Experience of Language Input across the Curriculum | | | Language Output from the Children in an Activity-Based Context | |
| --- | --- | --- | --- | --- |
| Activities and topics | Teacher's questions, instructions, and comments about: | Physical Response Activities | Vocabulary | Expressions and structures |
| making a Snapdragon | cutting and folding; spelling; playing *Snapdragon* | colour pick fold | *colours* first next last another mine yours his/hers | finished like this How do you spell . . . ? heads or tails I like/don't like . . . |

Table 2

| Lesson 1 Preparation Activities | Lesson 2 Main Activity: Making a Snapdragon | Lesson 3 Follow Up Activities |
|---|---|---|
| Warm Up: writing letter shapes on a friend's back | Warm Up: Action Game: use Class Cassette Unit 2, Part 2 (follow Procedure 2) | Warm Up: the children make alphabet letters with their bodies |
| Check Homework: Picture Dictionaries; colour in *star 4* | Check Homework: play *Alphabet bingo* | Check Homework: play *Snapdragon* |
| Presenting New Language: spellings | Activity: the children make and play with the Snapdragon on Unit 5 Activity Page (Student's Book page 31) | Language Practice: describing how they made their Snapdragons |
| Game: play *Alphabet bingo* | Language Practice: *How do you spell . . .?* use Class Cassette Unit 5, Part 1 | Unit 5 Workpage (Student's Book page 11): – use Home Cassette, Unit 5, Parts A and B |
| Review: Unit 2 – family vocabulary | Review: the children sing *One, two, buckle my shoe* – use Class Cassette Unit 2, Part 5 | Song: the children sing *One finger, one thumb* – use Class Cassette Unit 5, Part 3 |
| Homework: find and glue alphabet letters into own Picture Dictionary | Homework: glue in a Snapdragon envelope onto Student's Book page 10 | Homework: finish off Workpage (Student's Book page 11) |
| Round Up: play *Heads or tails* | Round Up: play *Heads or tails* | Round Up: play story game using vocabulary from Unit 2 |

*Note:* The review Unit is Unit 2.

# Lesson 1
# Preparation Activities

## PREPARING YOUR LESSON

– Bring in your colour and word sets of flash cards for the colours: *pink, blue, yellow, green.*

– Prepare simple flash cards for the alphabet.

alphabet song
photo copies p100 T for Ts

## WARM UP

How do you spell your name?

- group formation activity
- reviewing and consolidating the alphabet
- friendship activity

alphabet dictation

Writing letter shapes on a partner's back.

i. Demonstrate the activity with S1. You sit behind S1 and write a letter of the alphabet on his or her back with your finger. S1 must guess the letter and write it on the palm of your hand. You change roles and repeat the activity.

ii. Organise the children into pairs. S1 sits behind S2. Pairs do the finger writing activity.

iii. The children change roles, then partners and repeat the activity.

## CHECK HOMEWORK

a) Check the children have filed the items correctly in their new Picture Dictionaries, then ask them to talk about the pages in their Dictionary.

i. You give the example. Point to your *colours* page as you speak:
T: *This is my colours page. This is blue. This is red. This is green.*

ii. You repeat your description, leaving out key words. The class says the missing words.
T: *This is my . . .*
Ss: *Colours page . . .*
T: *This is . . .*
Ss: *Green . . . etc.*

iii. S1 comes to the front of the class. S1 points to the items on his or her *colours* page. The class describes them. Repeat this activity with a new S1.

colour letters on alphabet according to similar sound

iv. Organise the children into groups of three or four. The children take turns to describe the content of pages in their new Picture Dictionaries to their group. (Also encourage them to check each other's *spellings.*) You go round and help with the language. Whenever feasible say a complete description while the children are listening. Then let them try. Encourage student-to-student correction rather than allowing the children merely to repeat line by line after you.

v. Choose and encourage the children to talk about Dictionary pages to the rest of the class. Allow errors. Don't correct the children as they speak. Encourage all attempts. If needed, when a child has finished, repeat your example. Get other children to try.

b) Grading Unit 4.

i. Show your completed pages for Unit 4. As for previous Units, ask the children what colour (grade) you deserve for your work. Turn to the *star chart* on the inside back cover of the book. Abide by the class decision on your grade, and colour in *star 4* on the star chart.

ii. Ask the children to work in pairs. The children colour in their partner's *star* for this Unit. If there is any dispute, ask another child to be the final judge of grade.

iii. Check that parents have signed their children's Workpage.

## PRESENTING NEW LANGUAGE

- learning the spellings of the colours on the Snapdragon
- using the expression: *How do you spell . . . ?* || colours

Teach how to spell the colours on the Snapdragon. Use your flash cards for the colours as teaching aids.

i. Organise the class into a semi-circle. Give out the four *word* flash cards of the colours to four children. You say the colours as you give out the cards. The children listen only.

ii. You say the colours. The children hold up the appropriate flash card. They don't speak.

iii. You say the colours. The children with the flash cards hold them up. The remainder of the class points to or touches something of that colour. They don't speak at this stage.

iv. Play *Match the colour to the spelling.*
Display your *colour* flash cards on the floor or your desk. Show a *word* flash card. Ask the children to find and hold up the matching colour.

v. Divide the class into two teams. Give out the colour flash cards to Team 1, and the word cards to Team 2. Teams display their flash cards. You say a colour. The first child to put his or her hand up and identify the correct colour, either the spelling or the colour itself, scores a point. The child who gets the correct answer says the next colour.

vi. Repeat the activity. This time you spell the colour. The first child to touch or hold up the correct answer scores a team point.
T: *Y. . .e. . .l. . .l. . .o. . .w   . . . spells . . .*

vii. Focus on the question: *How do you spell , . . ?*
Organise the class in groups of three or four. Appoint one leader for each group. Use Unit 5, Part 1 on the Class Cassette. Play the Cassette. Pause the Cassette after each question, rewind and play the question again, encouraging the leaders to ask the questions with the Cassette. Group members answer. Don't correct errors at this stage.

**Tapescript**   *Play ss, repeat qs*
Unit 5, Part 1. *Listen and spell these words.*
1. How do you spell yellow?
2. How do you spell blue?
3. How do you spell green?      *then ss ans*
4. How do you spell pink?

viii. Groups change leaders and repeat the activity. You go round the class and help with the language if needed. As in previous Units, don't encourage the children merely to repeat after you. Give the children complete examples to listen to, leave the group, and allow them time to practise. Return later to check on results.

## GAME

• consolidating the letters of the alphabet
• listening skills

Play *Alphabet bingo.*

i. Write up the alphabet on the board.

ii. Each child writes six alphabet letters on a piece of paper.

iii. You put your alphabet flash cards into a bag or box and take them out one at a time, calling them out as you do so.

iv. The first child to get all six letters called out says BINGO.

v. Play the game again. Choose children as bingo callers.

## REVIEW

Review Unit 2.

a) Review the language.

i.   Organise the class into two teams.

ii.  The children open their books at Unit 2. You ask questions. Correct answers score a team point. For example:
T: *Is this Minnie's sister?*
S: *No. (Minnie's mum.)*
T: *Who's this?*
S: *Donald's dad . . . etc.*

b) Team Challenge.
Organise the class into two teams. The children from each team take turns to ask opposing team members questions about their Unit 2 pages. Correct questions and answers score team points. If there are errors, when a child has finished, you ask a *bonus points* question, thus giving the class another chance to listen to a correct example of the question.

c) Group work.

i.   Organise the class into groups of three. Assign roles for members of each group: S1 is the checker, S2 looks at S3's book and asks questions for one minute, S3 answers. S1 listens and scores one point for each correct question and answer. (Demonstrate the activity first with one group of children.)

ii.  The children change roles and repeat the activity.

## HOMEWORK

Ask the children to find (in comics, magazines, etc.) and cut out the alphabet letters. Ask them to glue these letters onto the *alphabet* page in their Picture Dictionary. Demonstrate the meaning of your instructions with your own Dictionary.

## ROUND UP  *coin rubbings*

Play *Heads or tails.* Flip a coin.
T: *Heads or tails? Hands up if you think it's heads. Sorry it's tails. If you didn't put your hands up you can go.*

# Lesson 2
# Making a Snapdragon

## PREPARING YOUR LESSON

– Prepare a giant size Snapdragon for demonstration purposes. The instructions are on page 31 of the Student's Book.

– Prepare your Activity Page Snapdragon in advance.

## WARM UP

Use the Action Game on the Class Cassette (Unit 2, Part 2). Follow Action Game Procedure 2 on page 18.

*Tapescript*
*Unit 2, Part 2. Listen and do the actions.*
Stand over there, please. Back a bit. Good. Now smile. Say cheese. Thank you.

## CHECK HOMEWORK

i. Ask the children to show you their *alphabet page*. Find out which children have the largest and smallest size letters.

ii. Play one game of alphabet bingo. Use the same procedure as in Lesson 1 of this Unit.

## ACTIVITY

Making a Snapdragon.

i. Organise the class into groups of three or four. Double check everyone has easy access to scissors and a ruler. Appoint a *tidy monitor* for each group.

ii. Ask the children to find the Snapdragon on page 31 of their *early bird* books.

iii. Show the end product: a completed Snapdragon. Then, using your giant Snapdragon, show them how to make the Snapdragon, step by step. Give the instructions one step at a time. Make sure that all the children follow your instructions as you say them.

iv. Teach them how to play the game by demonstrating with S1. Start with the Snapdragon closed. When S1 has chosen a colour, you open and close the Snapdragon as you spell the word. S1 then chooses a number from inside the Snapdragon. You open and close the Snapdragon as you count it out. S1 then chooses another

number and you reveal the food item underneath. Teach the language as you play the game. For example:
T: *Pick a colour.*
S1: *Blue.*
T: *b...l...u...e. Now pick a number.*
S1: *5.*
T: *1...2...3...4...5. Pick another number.*
S1: *7.*
T: *You get a...hot dog. Here you are...*

v. Choose two children to demonstrate the game. S1 plays with S2. You help with the language. The other children observe.

vi. Pairwork. You go round the class and help with the language if needed. As before, don't encourage the children merely to repeat after you. Give the children complete examples to listen to, leave the group, and allow them time to practise. Return later to check on results.

## LANGUAGE PRACTICE

a) Consolidate the expression: *How do you spell...?* Use Unit 5, Part 1 on the Class Cassette.

i. You play the Cassette. Choose children to answer.

*Tapescript*
*Unit 5, Part 1. Listen and spell these words.*
1. How do you spell yellow?
2. How do you spell blue?
3. How do you spell green?
4. How do you spell pink?

ii. Encourage the children to ask you the questions, with help from the Cassette.

iii. Organise the children into pairs. S1 of each pair is going to ask the questions. Play the Cassette. Pause the Cassette after each question, rewind and play the question again, encouraging S1 to ask the questions with the Cassette. S2 answers. Don't correct errors at this stage. You go round the class and help with the language if needed.

iv. The children change roles and repeat the activity without the Cassette. As before, don't encourage the children merely to repeat after you. Give the children complete examples to listen to, leave the group, and allow them time to practise. Return later to check on results.

b) Spelling Challenge (focus on use of *spells*).

i. Organise the class into groups of four. Appoint a leader for each group. Play Unit 5, Part 2 on the Class Cassette. Leaders choose children to answer.

✳ *Tapescript* ○–8
*Unit 5, Part 2. Listen, and say the right word.*
1. g. . .r. . .e. . .e. . .n           . . . spells . . .
2. b. . .l. . .u. . .e                 . . . spells . . .
3. p. . .i. . .n. . .k                 . . . spells . . .
4. y. . .e. . .l. . .l. . .o. . .w     . . . spells . . .

ii. Repeat the activity. This time pause the Cassette after each question, rewind and play the question again, encouraging the leaders to ask the questions with the Cassette. Group members answer. Don't correct errors at this stage.

iii. Change leaders. Repeat the activity without the Cassette. Encourage leaders to ask the spelling of other words.

## REVIEW

Practise the song from Unit 2, Part 5 on the Class Cassette *One, two, buckle my shoe*. Sing this song as a round.

i.   Divide the class into four groups.

ii.  Group 1 sings the first line (*One, two, buckle my shoe*). The remaining groups listen.

iii. Group 1 continues with the second line (*Three, four, knock at the door*). Group 2 sings the first line. The remaining groups listen.

iv. Group 1 continues with the third line. Group 2 with the second line. Group 3 sings the first line. The remaining group listens. Continue until Group 4 has finished singing.

*Tapescript*
*Unit 2, Part 5. Listen and join in.*
One, two, buckle my shoe.
Three, four, knock at the door.
Five, six, pick up sticks.
Seven, eight, put them straight.
Nine, ten, start again.

## HOMEWORK

Ask the children to glue an envelope onto page 10 of their *early bird* books and to decorate it. They keep their Snapdragons safe in this envelope. They also glue the *picture instructions* for the Snapdragon onto the space provided.

## ROUND UP

Play *Heads or tails* again. Follow the same procedure as in Lesson 1 of this Unit.

# Lesson 3
# Follow Up Activities

## PREPARING YOUR LESSON

Prepare your Workpage, page 11 of the Student's Book for demonstration purposes.

## WARM UP
✳
Make alphabet letters with your body.
The children work in pairs or groups. You give the instructions. They make letters with their own bodies, or their partners' bodies or as a group. For example:
T: *Make your partner into a letter 'a' . . . etc.*

## CHECK HOMEWORK

Ask the children to show you that their envelopes have been correctly glued onto page 10 of their *early bird* books. Get the children to play one game of *Snapdragon.*

## LANGUAGE PRACTICE

*   describing how the children made their Snapdragons (*Note:* The past tense is introduced in context, but not extensively taught.)
*   using gestures to explain a task

Ask the children to explain how they made their Snapdragons.

i.   Unfold your Snapdragon in advance. Then set up the *language model* by re-making your Snapdragon step by step, describing what you did after each step. For example:
T: *I made my Snapdragon like this. First I folded this, like this. Next I folded this, like this . . . Next I did this. Last I did this. Finished.*

ii.  You repeat your description, leaving out key words. The class says the missing words.
T: *I made my Snapdragon like . . .*
Ss: *This.*
T: *First, I folded this . . .*
Ss: *Like this . . . etc.*

iii. S1 comes to the front of the class. S1 shows how he or she made the Snapdragon. The class describes the steps as S1 does the actions. Repeat this activity with a new S1.

iv. Organise the children into groups of three or four. The children take turns to explain how they made their Snapdragon to their group. You go round and help with the language. Whenever feasible say a complete description while the children are listening. Then let them try. Encourage student-to-student correction rather than allowing the children merely to repeat line by line after you.

v. Choose and encourage children to describe how they made their Snapdragon to the rest of the class. Allow errors. Don't correct the children as they speak. Encourage all attempts. If needed, when a child has finished, repeat your example description.

## WORKPAGE

• recording work done in this Unit
• reviewing and consolidating language from this Unit

Complete the Workpage, Student's Book page 11. Use Unit 5, Parts A and B on the Home Cassette.

i. Organise the class into groups of three or four.

ii. Demonstrate how to do Part A. Play Unit 5, Part A on the Home Cassette. When the children understand what to do, play the Cassette again. The children write the spelling of the colours in their books.

*Tapescript*
*Unit 5, Part A. Listen. Write in the spellings.*
1. How do you spell yellow?
2. How do you spell blue?
3. How do you spell green?
4. How do you spell pink?

iii. Demonstrate how to do Part B. The children colour in the boxes according to the instructions on the Cassette. Use Unit 5, Part B on the Home Cassette.

*Tapescript*
*Unit 5, Part B. Listen. Colour the boxes.*
1. g. . .r. . .e. . .e. . .n        . . . spells . . .
2. b. . .l. . .u. . .e              . . . spells . . .
3. p. . .i. . .n. . .k              . . . spells . . .
4. y. . .e. . .l. . .l. . .o. . .w  . . . spells . . .

## SONG

Introduce *One finger, one thumb* using Unit 5, Part 3 on the Class Cassette. Make sure the children use lots of gestures as they sing.

*Tapescript*
*Unit 5, Part 3. Listen and join in.*
One finger, one thumb, keep moving.
One finger, one thumb, keep moving.
One finger, one thumb, keep moving.
And off to town we go.
One finger, one thumb, one arm, keep moving.
One finger, one thumb, one arm, keep moving.
One finger, one thumb, one arm, keep moving.
And off to town we go.
One finger, one thumb, one arm, one leg, keep moving.
One finger, one thumb, one arm, one leg, keep moving.
One finger, one thumb, one arm, one leg, keep moving.
And off to town we go.
One finger, one thumb, one arm, one leg, one nod of the head, keep moving.
One finger, one thumb, one arm, one leg, one nod of the head, keep moving.
One finger, one thumb, one arm, one leg, one nod of the head, keep moving.
And off to town we go.
One finger, one thumb, one arm, one leg, one nod of the head, stand up, sit down, keep moving.
One finger, one thumb, one arm, one leg, one nod of the head, stand up, sit down, keep moving.
One finger, one thumb, one arm, one leg, one nod of the head, stand up, sit down, keep moving.
And off to town we go.
One finger, one thumb, one arm, one leg, one nod of the head, stand up, turn round, sit down, keep moving.
One finger, one thumb, one arm, one leg, one nod of the head, stand up, turn round, sit down, keep moving.
One finger, one thumb, one arm, one leg, one nod of the head, stand up, turn round, sit down, keep moving.
And off to town we go.

## HOMEWORK

Assign page 11, Parts C and D of the *early bird* book for homework. Encourage the children to ask their parents to sign their completed Workpage.

## ROUND UP

- reviewing family and pets vocabulary
- group formation activity
- friendship and trust activity

Play a story game using *family* and *pets* as the key words.

i. Organise the class into two teams. The teams line up in front of the board, about 1 metre between the two lines. The children turn to face each other and form pairs with the child facing them.

ii. Pairs join hands and raise their arms, thus forming a sort of archway or tunnel.

iii. Assign each pair (S1 from Team 1 and S1 from Team 2) of children a family name: *mum, dad, brother, sister,* or a pet: *dog, cat, budgie, goldfish.* Make up a simple story which contains these words. When the children hear their word, they must race their partner under the arch of arms, to the back of the line, then back to their original places. Team mates shout: *Come on, come on,* as encouragement. First child back scores a team point.

*Example Story Script*
*One day last week, I went shopping with my **mum** and **dad** . . . I had to buy a red sweater for school. We waited at the bus stop. Suddenly, I saw a big white . . . **dog**. . . . The **dog** . . . was chasing a . . . **cat** . . . and my **mum** . . . said that she hated **dogs** and **cats** . . . etc.*

## EVALUATION

In terms of evaluation of this Unit, the following table can be used as a guide. You may photocopy and include it in your school record book. For simplicity, tick a column if you are satisfied with a child's performance; leave it blank if you are not happy. *Note:* The table is a guide, and a record to refer back to. It is not intended as a grade list.

| Name | Activity completed | Can play *Snapdragon* in English | Can understand your questions about spelling | Can ask how to spell English words | Can explain how to make the Snapdragon | Review: Successful recall of language from Unit 2 |
|---|---|---|---|---|---|---|
| | | | | | | |
| | | | | | | |
| | | | | | | |
| | | | | | | |
| | | | | | | |
| | | | | | | |
| | | | | | | |
| | | | | | | |

# Unit 6  Story Time

## INTRODUCTION

This is the first Cartoon Story Unit in the course. The aims of the Story Units are as follows:

– consolidating and reviewing language;

– introducing a wide range of new language;

– focusing on corporeal expression, spatial awareness, non-verbal communication;

– sequencing events in picture form;

– dramatising a dialogue;

– enjoying a story.

In addition to these general aims, Unit 6:

– focuses on emotions and feelings: *happiness, sadness, hunger, anger, surprise, fear, embarrassment, humour;*

– introduces the class to the dramatic expression of a dialogue;

– introduces the course characters Andy and Annie.

## Content and Format of Cartoon Story Pages

– The Cartoon Story Pages review and preview the key vocabulary from the course. They are introduced at regular intervals: Unit 6 in Book 1, and Units 1 and 11 in Book 2.

– The stories are presented in cartoon picture form. There is no written script in the student text.

– The children's comprehension of the story is gradually built up through a series of activities. These include physical response, sequencing of picture information, storytelling and drama.

– The children cut up the Cartoon Story Pages into individual cartoon pictures. The cartoon story for Unit 6 is printed on page 33.

– The frame outlines for each cartoon picture are printed in the main body of the *early bird* text. The outlines for Unit 6, for example, are printed on page 12.

– Once cut out, and as a final activity, the cartoon pictures are assembled, in the correct order, onto these outlines.

Table 1 (below) summarises the content of the Unit. Table 2 gives an outline of the key teaching steps.

## Table 1

| The Children's Experience of Language Input across the Curriculum | | | Language Output from the Children in an Activity-Based Context | |
|---|---|---|---|---|
| Activities and topics | Teacher's questions, instructions, and comments about: | Physical Response Activities | Vocabulary | Expressions and structures |
| cartoon story | identifying pictures; organising picture information; storytelling; acting and role play of the story | pick up squeeze open bite | Review | bald head Hi! lots and lots bites, puts opens, goes (present simple) |

**Table 2**

| Lesson 1<br>Preparation Activities | Lesson 2<br>Main Activity:<br>Story Time | Lesson 3<br>Follow Up Activities |
|---|---|---|
| Warm Up: play *Mirror statues* | Warm Up: Action Game: use Class Cassette Unit 6, Part 1 (follow Procedure 2) | Warm Up: Action Game: use Class Cassette Unit 6, Part 1 (follow Procedure 3) |
| Check Homework: colour in *star 5* in the star chart | Check Homework: review content of the cartoon story – use Class Cassette Unit 6, Part 2 | Check Homework: review Role Play from last lesson |
| Action Game: use Class Cassette Unit 6, Part 1 (follow Procedure 1) | Activity: story time – use Class Cassette Unit 6, Part 3 | Unit 6 Workpage (Student's Book page 13): use Home Cassette, Units 6, Parts A, B and C |
| Previewing the Cartoon Story: use Class Cassette Unit 6, Part 2; cut up Unit 6 Activity Page (Student's Book page 33) | Role Play: based on the story | Language Practice: narrating parts of the cartoon story |
| Review: Unit 3 – *What's this called in English?* | Homework: bring in drama props; glue in story lines | Game: play story game with *food* and *condiments* |
| Homework: glue cartoon pictures onto Student's Book page 12 | Round Up: the children sing *One finger, one thumb* – use Class Cassette Unit 5, Part 3 | Homework: the children teach their parents the Action Game for Unit 6; finish off Workpage (Student's Book page 13) |
| Round Up: the children sing *Head, body, legs and tail* – use Class Cassette Unit 3, Part 5 | | Round Up: play *Mirror statues* |

*Note:* The review Unit is Unit 3.

# Lesson 1
# Preparation Activities

## PREPARING FOR THE STORY UNIT

– Prepare flash cards for each of the cartoon pictures on page 33 of the Student's Book. For a small class, use photocopies of each cartoon picture, pasted onto thin card. For large classes, make enlarged photocopies for each picture. These can be coloured in by the children as an additional *preview activity*.

– Listen to the Class Cassette and read the story lines. Decide on useful props for the story. For example: ketchup, empty hamburger and french fries containers, paper serviettes, a hat or tie (for the bald man), a denim jacket or large shirt (Andy), a pair of braces or large sweater or scarf (Annie), a bow tie or paper hat (shop assistant).

## WARM UP

• introducing the *emotions* in the cartoon story
• introducing the vocabulary for emotions
• group formation activity
• encouraging accurate observation

Play *Mirror statues.*
Organise the class into pairs. You give instructions for:

*Draw adjs on board
fat thin
small big
old young*

– *happy/sad statues;*

– *surprised/angry statues;*

– *hungry / full of food statues. beautiful ugly*

For example:
T: *You're a happy statue. Make a happy face. Come on, you're happy. Now stand in a happy way. Show me you're happy . . . etc.*
The children work in pairs. S1 strikes a *happy* pose. S2 is the *mirror* and must copy S1 exactly. The children change roles, then partners and repeat the activity.

## CHECK HOMEWORK

i. Show your completed pages for Unit 5. As in previous Units, ask the children what colour (grade) you deserve for your work. Turn to the *star chart* on the inside back cover of the book. Abide by the class decision on your grade, and colour in *star 5* on the star chart.

ii. Ask the children to work in pairs. The children colour in their partner's *star* for this Unit. If there is any dispute, ask another child to be the final judge of grade.

iii. Check that parents have signed their children's Workpage.

## ACTION GAME

• active understanding of *eating a hamburger* language
• introducing language and context for the Cartoon Story
• group formation activity

Use Unit 6, Part 1 on the Class Cassette. This is the first time the children have played this game, so follow Action Game Procedure 1 on page 15.

*Tapescript*
*Unit 6, Part 1.  Listen and do the actions.*
Ready? Pick up the hamburger. Pick up the ketchup. Squeeze the ketchup on the hamburger. Now open your mouth and bite.

## PREVIEWING THE CARTOON STORY

• introducing the language and context for the story
• developing listening skills

i. Organise the class into a semi-circle.

ii. Use your flash cards of the cartoon pictures. Play Unit 6, Part 2 on the Class Cassette. Hold up or point to each cartoon picture or flash card as you play the Cassette. Also use gestures to help explain the meaning. The children watch and listen only at this stage.

*Tapescript*
*Unit 6, Part 2. Listen and hold up the right pictures.*
1. This is Andy.
2. This is Andy again.
3. This is a hamburger.
4. This is another hamburger.
5. These are french fries.
6. These are more french fries.
7. Andy asks for a yummy hamburger.
8. This is the ketchup.
9. Andy puts lots of ketchup on the hamburger.
10. This is Annie.
11. This is Annie again.
12. Annie says 'Hi' to Andy. Andy jumps.
13. Oh no! The ketchup goes all over the man.

iii. Play the Cassette again. Hold up two flash cards for each story line, one of which is the correct picture. The children point to the correct one.

iv. Mix your flash cards up. Lay them on the floor or your desk. Play the Cassette again. Ask the children to find and hold up the correct pictures.

v. Organise the class into groups of three or four. Make sure all the children have access to a pair of scissors. Ask the children to turn to page 33 of their *early bird* books.

vi. Ask them to cut up their cartoon pages. Ask the children who finish first to help slower classmates.
   - Organise the children into pairs. The pairs mix up their pictures and lay them face down. Play the Cassette again. The children take turns in finding and holding up the correct pictures to their partners.
   - Say the story lines again. This time the children pick up the correct cartoon pictures and put them in their *bits and pieces* envelopes on the inside front cover of their books.

## REVIEW

- reviewing language from Unit 3
- using the expressions:
  *What's this called in English?*
  *What are these called in English?*

Review Unit 3. Encourage the children to ask each other questions about beetles.

a) Review the language.

   i. Organise the class into two teams.

   ii. The children open their books at Unit 3. You ask questions. Correct answers score a team point. For example:
   T: *Look at my beetle. Tell me. What's this called in English?*
   S: *Head.*
   T: *And what are these called in English?*
   S: *Legs . . . etc.*

b) Team Challenge.
   Organise the class into two teams. The children from each team take turns to ask opposing team members questions about their Unit 3 pages. Correct questions and answers score team points. If there are errors, when a child has finished, you ask a *bonus points* question, thus giving the class another chance to listen to a correct example of the question.

c) Group work.

   i. Organise the class into groups of three. Assign roles for members of each group: S1 is the checker, S2 looks at S3's book and asks questions for one minute, S3 answers. S1 listens and awards one point for each correct question and answer.

   ii. The children change roles and repeat the activity. You go round the class and help with the language if needed. Encourage the children to ask other questions about the beetles, and to describe the beetles to their group. As before, don't let the children merely repeat after you. Give the children complete examples to listen to, leave the group, and allow them time to practise. Return later to check on results.

## HOMEWORK

Ask the children to glue the cartoon pictures in the correct order onto page 12 in their *early bird* books.

## ROUND UP

Review the song from Unit 3 on the Class Cassette: *Head, body, legs and tail.*

# Lesson 2
# Story Time

## PREPARING YOUR LESSON

- Prepare and read the story script (Unit 6, Part 3 on the Class Cassette) in advance.

- Bring in any useful props (see Preparation for Lesson 1 of this Unit).

- Glue your cartoon pictures from page 33 of the Student's Book onto page 12.

## WARM UP

Use the Action Game on the Class Cassette (Unit 6, Part 1). This is the second time the children have played this game, so follow Action Game Procedure 2 on page 18.

*Tapescript*
*Unit 6, Part 1. Listen and do the actions.*
Ready? Pick up the hamburger. Pick up the ketchup. Squeeze the ketchup on the hamburger. Now open your mouth and bite.

## CHECK HOMEWORK

i. Organise the class into groups of three or four. The children open their books at page 12. You play the story lines on the Class Cassette (Unit 6, Part 2). Pause the Cassette after each story line, rewind and play the line again, encouraging S1 of each group to speak with the Cassette. Other children in the group touch the correct picture, and help S1 with any problems after he or she has finished speaking. Don't correct errors at this stage.

ii. The children change roles and repeat the activity. You go round the class and help with the language if needed. As in previous Units, don't encourage the children merely to repeat after you. Give the children complete examples to listen to, leave the group, and allow them time to practise. Return later to check on results.

## ACTIVITY

There are five main stages:

a) Confirming the overall context and meaning of the story using flash cards of the story pictures.

   i. You give out the flash cards of the story to the children. They come to the front of the class and display them in the correct order.

   ii. Organise the class into a semi-circle. Point to each flash card in turn and confirm the key vocabulary, locations and characters. Give incomplete information. The children listen and complete the gaps in your descriptions. For example:
   T: *Look at this picture. This is a picture of . . .*
   S: *Andy.*
   T: *And this is a picture of a . . .*
   S: *Hamburger.*
   T: *What sort of hamburger? A big hamburger or a small hamburger?*
   S: *Big . . . etc.*

b) Identifying the movement and action in more detail. Use a PR (Physical Response) Activity as a means of conveying the key actions and movement in the story.

   i. Set up the key locations in your classroom for the action in the story: *the entrance to the hamburger store; the store counter; the cash desk.*

   ii. Use your props with the following script:
   *Andy walks into a hamburger store. He's very, very hungry. He orders a super big hamburger and a bag of super big french fries. Andy puts lots and lots of ketchup on the hamburger. He opens his mouth . . .*
   *Annie comes quietly into the store. She walks behind Andy. She puts her hand on Andy's shoulder. Andy jumps. He bites the hamburger very hard. Whoosh. The ketchup goes all over the man with the bald head. The man is very, very angry.*
   - You say the script and demonstrate the actions. Wear a jacket when you play Andy; a scarf when you play Annie; a hat when you play the bald man. The children listen and watch only (no speaking).
   - Divide the class into three groups. Group 1 plays Andy; Group 2 plays Annie; Group 3 plays the bald man; Group 4 plays the hamburger store assistant. Say the script again. You and the children do the actions together. The children don't speak.
   - Say the script again. You watch the children. One child from each of the groups does the actions. The remainder of the groups observe.
   - Say the script again leaving information gaps for the children to complete.
   During this activity, encourage the children to move around the class and use lots of gestures to denote the movement and action in the story.

c) Telling and dramatising the story.

   i. Organise the class so that they are comfortable and can see you and the flash cards. Don't start the story until everyone is ready.

   ii. Tell the complete story (see Story Script below). Use exaggerated gestures, props and sound effects to enhance your reading, and the children's enjoyment of the story.

### Story Script

*One day, Andy went to town. He went to a hamburger store. He was starving. He asked for a super big hamburger, super big french fries and lots and lots of ketchup. Yum.*
*Andy picked up the hamburger and opened his mouth wide. Suddenly he felt a hand on his shoulder. Andy jumped with surprise. He squeezed the hamburger hard. Oh no! The ketchup went all over the man with the bald head.*

   iii. Tell the story again. The children do the actions and gestures.

   iv. Use Unit 6, Part 3 on the Class Cassette. Play the Cassette. Stop the Cassette at the missing words. The children say the missing words.

### Tapescript

*Unit 6, Part 3. Listen to the story. Say the missing words.*
One day, Andy went to town. He went to a hamburger store. He was starving. He asked for a super big .........., super big .......... and lots and lots of .......... Yum. Andy picked up the hamburger and opened his mouth wide. Suddenly he felt a .......... on his shoulder. Andy jumped with surprise. He squeezed the hamburger hard. Oh no! The .......... went all over the man with the bald head.

d) Using *nonsense* and *missing* words.
Tell the story again. This time miss out other words or make deliberate mistakes. The children say the missing words or correct your mistakes. For example:
*One day, **a bald man** went to town. He went to a **department** store. He was .......... He asked for a super big **hot dog**, super big **Greek** fries and lots and lots of **mustard**. Yum.*
*Andy .......... the hamburger and opened his **hand** wide. Suddenly he felt a hand on his .......... Andy jumped with surprise. He .......... the hamburger hard. Oh no! The ketchup went all over **Annie**.*

e) Writing the key lines for the cartoon pictures. This is an optional activity for children over nine years old only.

   i. The children sit in groups of four. Choose four cartoon pictures. You write up the story lines for these pictures on the board. Miss out one or two words in each line. Put these missing words in a box beside the story lines. For example:

*This .... Andy.*

*.... is another hamburger.*

*Andy puts .... of ketchup on the ....*

*Oh no! The .... goes all over the ....*

| |
|---|
| *lots and lots* |
| *is* |
| *ketchup* |
| *man* |
| *This* |
| *hamburger* |

   ii. You say each (complete) line, touching the words as you speak.

   iii. Ask two children to come to the board. You say each line (in random order). They touch the correct words as you speak.

   iv. The children copy these story lines onto a piece of paper. Encourage the group members to check each other's work. When finished, the children put their papers into their *bits and pieces* envelopes. (See Homework below.)

## ROLE PLAY

- allowing the children the freedom to improvise
- asking for food in English
- using the expressions: *please; thank you; here you are; sorry*

   i. Set the scene for the role play of the story. Establish where the store entrance is, where the counter is, where the characters are, and where they move to.

   ii. Choose children to take the roles of the four characters. The remainder of the class observes.

   iii. The children act out what happened in the store. You speak appropriate dialogue lines as the children mime their roles. Ask the remaining children to listen carefully to your dialogue lines. The children don't speak at this stage.

   iv. Choose four new children to take the character roles. Repeat the activity. The non-acting children listen carefully to your dialogue.

   v. Divide the class up into groups of four. Groups rehearse the scene. You go round the class and help with the language if needed. Encourage changes in the dialogue. Discourage the children from merely repeating after you. Give the children complete examples to listen to, leave the group, and allow them time to rehearse. Return later to check on results.

vi. Groups perform their scene for the rest of the class. This is a free stage. Don't correct errors.

*Example Dialogue*
Andy: *Big hamburger, and french fries, please.*
Man 1: *Here you are.*
Andy: *Ketchup please.*
Man 1: *Here you are.*
Andy: *How much please?*
Man 1: *$2.00.*
Andy: *Here you are.*
Annie: *Hi Andy.*
Andy: *Oh no!!!*
Man 2: *Grrrrrr.*
Andy: *Sorry ...!*

## HOMEWORK

i. Ask the children to bring in drama props for acting out the story next lesson.

ii. This is an optional activity for children over nine years old. Ask the children to glue their story lines onto the appropriate cartoon pictures stuck on page 12. Demonstrate what to do.
   – Cut up the story lines into four strips. One strip contains one story line.
   – Glue about 1 cm. of each strip onto its corresponding cartoon picture. In this way the story line is attached to the correct picture, and can be raised if necessary to show the complete picture.

## ROUND UP

Review the song from Unit 5, Part 3 on the Class Cassette: *One finger, one thumb*.

# Lesson 3
# Follow Up Activities

## PREPARING YOUR LESSON

– Prepare your Workpage, Student's Book page 13, for demonstration purposes.

– Bring in *salt, pepper, ketchup* and *mustard*.

– Bring in your flash cards for the cartoon pictures.

## WARM UP

• group formation
• consolidating and using the language of the Action Game

Use the Action Game on the Class Cassette (Unit 6, Part 1). This is the third time the children have played this game, so follow Action Game Procedure 3 on page 20.

## CHECK HOMEWORK AND REVIEW

The children act out the story again:

i. Collect in and sort the various props brought in.

ii. Organise the class into new groups of four. Appoint a group leader for each group. Groups discuss what props they want, and group leaders collect them.

iii. Review the dialogue(s) used last lesson. Ask one group to mime their scene while you improvise a simple dialogue as they act.

iv. Groups rehearse their scenes. You go round the class and help with the language.

v. Groups perform their scene for the rest of the class. This is a free stage. Don't correct errors.

## WORKPAGE

Complete the Workpage, Student's Book page 13. Use Unit 6, Parts A, B and C on the Home Cassette.

a) Review how to do the *Teach your parents* activity at home[1]. Use Unit 6, Part A on the Home Cassette. Do a role play for the *Teach your parents* situation. Choose two children. S1 is the parent. S2 is him- or herself:

---

[1] This activity may be too difficult for younger children. With a younger class, you will need to do a higher percentage of the Workpage activities in class time.

i. Ask S2 to give the class a short practical demonstration on how to use the cassette player. Encourage S2 to use the expression *like this* as he or she explains.

ii. Role play: S2 plays the Cassette and demonstrates the actions on the Cassette. S1 (the parent) watches and listens.

iii. S2 plays the Cassette again and does the actions with S1 (the parent).

iv. S2 gives the instructions with the Cassette. S1 (the parent) does the actions. S2 watches.

*Tapescript*
*Unit 6, Part A. Listen. Teach your parents.*
Ready? Pick up the hamburger. Pick up the ketchup. Squeeze the ketchup on the hamburger. Now open your mouth and bite.

b) Do exercise B.

i. Organise the class into groups of three or four.

ii. Demonstrate what to do. Show your own Student's Book page 13 then play the Home Cassette (Unit 6, Part B). The children write the missing words in their books. Encourage the children to check each other's work and to help each other.

*Tapescript*
*Unit 6, Part B. Listen again. Write in the missing words.*
Ready? Pick up the hamburger. Pick up the ketchup. Squeeze the ketchup on the hamburger. Now open your mouth and bite.

c) Demonstrate how to do Part C. Use Unit 6, Part C on the Home Cassette. Do the first example with the class. Assign the rest for homework.

*Tapescript*
*Unit 6, Part C. Listen to the story. Draw the missing pictures. Write the missing words under your pictures. Colour in your pictures.*
One day, Andy went to town. He went to a hamburger store. He was starving. He asked for a super big .........., super big .......... and lots and lots of .......... Yum. Andy picked up the hamburger and opened his mouth wide. Suddenly he felt a .......... on his shoulder. Andy jumped with surprise. He squeezed the hamburger hard. Oh no! The .......... went all over the man with the bald head.

## LANGUAGE PRACTICE

• reviewing and narrating the story

a) Review the story line for each cartoon picture.

i. Display your flash cards in random order. Play Unit 6, Part 2 on the Class Cassette. Ask the children to choose and hold up the correct cartoon picture or flash card as you play the Cassette.

*Tapescript*
*Unit 6, Part 2. Listen and hold up the right pictures.*
1. This is Andy.
2. This is Andy again.
3. This is a hamburger.
4. This is another hamburger.
5. These are french fries.
6. These are more french fries.
7. Andy asks for a yummy hamburger.
8. This is the ketchup.
9. Andy puts lots of ketchup on the hamburger.
10. This is Annie.
11. This is Annie again.
12. Annie says 'Hi' to Andy. Andy jumps.
13. Oh no! The ketchup goes all over the man.

ii. Ask the children to number the cartoon pictures, which they have glued in their books on page 12.

b) Encourage the children to narrate and act out part of the cartoon story.

i. You demonstrate what to do. Choose S1 to act out your narration. The rest of the class listens and watches. For example:
T: *Andy puts lots of ketchup . . . on the hamburger, like this.*
S1 does the actions.
T: *Andy bites the hamburger, like this.*
S1 does the actions.
T: *The ketchup goes like this. Whoosh.*
S1 does the actions.

ii. You repeat your narration, leaving out key words. The class says the missing words. S1 does the actions.
T: *Andy puts lots of .......... on the .......... like ..........*
Class: *Ketchup . . . hamburger . . . this.*
S1 does the actions.
T: *Andy . . . the hamburger . . . this . . . etc.*

iii. Organise the children into groups of three or four. Groups practise. S1 in each group takes the role of narrator, S2 and S3 do the actions, S4 observes and comments on performance. You go round and help with the language.

Whenever feasible go through the complete narration while the children are listening. Then let them try. Encourage student-to-student correction within the group, rather than allowing the children merely to repeat line by line after you.

iv. Choose and encourage groups to demonstrate to the rest of the class. Allow errors. Don't correct the children as they speak. Encourage all attempts. If needed, when a group has finished, repeat your own narration. Get other groups to try.

## GAME

- consolidating *food* vocabulary
- introducing *condiment* vocabulary
- group formation activity
- friendship and trust activity

Play a story game using *food* and *condiments* as the key words.

a) Introduce the condiments: *ketchup, salt, pepper, mustard*. Use real items.

i. Organise the class into a semi-circle. Hand out the condiments, naming each condiment as you hand it over.

ii. Name each condiment. The child holding that condiment must hold it up. The remaining children must do an *action* for the condiment. For example: *shake* for the salt, *squeeze* for the ketchup, and so on.

b) Play the story game.

i. Organise the class into two teams. The teams line up in front of the board with about 1 metre between the two lines. The children turn to face each other and form pairs with the children facing them.

ii. Pairs join hands and raise their arms, thus forming a sort of archway or tunnel.

iii. Assign each pair (S1 from Team 1 and S1 from Team 2) of children a food: *hamburger, hot dog, french fries*, or a condiment: *ketchup, salt, pepper, mustard*. Make up a simple story that contains these words. When the children hear their word, they must race their partner under the arch of arms, to the back of the line, then back to their original places. Team mates shout: *Come on, come on*, as encouragement. First child back scores a team point.

***Example Story Script***
*I went to McDonald's yesterday with my friend, Julie. Julie ordered* **french fries**. *I ordered a* **hamburger**. *I put lots and lots of* **ketchup** *on my* **hamburger**. *Julie put lots of* **salt** *on her* **french fries** ... *etc.*

## HOMEWORK

The children teach their parents the Action Game for this Unit. They also complete page 13, Part C of the *early bird* book. Encourage the children to ask their parents to sign their completed Workpage.

## ROUND UP

Play *Mirror statues*. Refer back to the Warm Up section for Lesson 1 of this Unit for the procedure. Allow the *happiest/saddest/angriest* pairs of statues to leave the class first.

## EVALUATION

In terms of evaluation of this Unit, the following table can be used as a guide. You may photocopy and include it in your school record book. For simplicity, tick a column if you are satisfied with a child's performance; leave it blank if you are not happy. *Note:* the table is a guide, and a record to refer back to. It is not intended as a grade list.

| Name | Has participated actively in the storytelling | Can give the PR instructions for this Unit | Can respond to the key vocabulary for this Unit | Has participated actively in the Role Play | Can give brief narration of key actions in the story |
|---|---|---|---|---|---|
| | | | | | |
| | | | | | |
| | | | | | |
| | | | | | |

67

# Unit 7    Joining the Dots

## INTRODUCTION

This Unit reviews language learned so far, and extends the children's knowledge in English of *numbers*, *adjectives* and *body parts*. The Unit deals with the theme of *elephants* and focuses on:

– drawing and colouring elephants;

– main parts of an elephant's body;

– studying, observing and describing elephants.

In addition, the dot number drawing encourages the children to:

– use numbers above 30;

– count in tens;

– compare *-teen* (16, 17, etc.) numbers and *-ty* (20, 30, etc.) numbers;

– explain simple arithmetic in English.

Through the practical activities in Unit 7, the children will:

– play number games in English;

– teach each other *simple arithmetic* in English;

– use *body parts* vocabulary;

– use *numbers 0–100*;

– use *is/are* to describe elephants;

– use the *present simple* form of *action verbs* to describe an elephant's habits;

– use *have/has* to describe elephants;

– use *adjectives* to describe elephants;

– consolidate their active recognition of a wide range of question forms in English.

Table 1 (below) summarises the content of the Unit. Table 2 gives an outline of the key teaching steps.

## Table 1

| The Children's Experience of Language Input across the Curriculum | | | Language Output from the Children in an Activity-Based Context | |
|---|---|---|---|---|
| Activities and topics | Teacher's questions, instructions, and comments about: | Physical Response Activities | Vocabulary | Expressions and structures |
| dot picture; facts about elephants | numbers; drawing and colouring; parts of the body; information about elephants | stand up come here pick up put down say join | teeth trunk ears right left numbers 20–100 its/their | please thank you plus/minus  eats, weighs, lives, equals (present simple) |

**Table 2**

| Lesson 1<br>Preparation Activities | Lesson 2<br>Main Activity:<br>Joining the Dots | Lesson 3<br>Follow Up Activities |
|---|---|---|
| Warm Up: play *Chinese whispers* with numbers | Warm Up: Action Game: use Class Cassette Unit 7, Part 2 (follow Procedure 2) | Warm Up: Action Game: use Class Cassette Unit 7, Part 2 (follow Procedure 3) |
| Check Homework: colour in *star 6* | Check Homework: display and identify *the hands* | Check Homework: feedback on elephants |
| Presenting New Language: review and develop Unit 3 (numbers): *-teen* and *-ty* | Activity: join the dots and colour the picture on Unit 7 Activity Page (Student's Book page 14) | Language Practice: describing elephants |
| Game: play *Simon says* – focus on *left* and *right* | Language Practice: question and answer work on elephants | Review: Unit 3; working with the value of coins |
| Action Game: use Class Cassette Unit 7, Part 2 (follow Procedure 1) | Review: Unit 3 – describing mini-beasts | Unit 7 Workpage (Student's Book page 15): use Home Cassette Unit 7, Parts A, B and C |
| Homework: draw round left and right hands | Homework: find out facts about elephants | Homework: finish off Workpage (Student's Book page 15) |
| Round Up: the children make *team numbers* | Round Up: the children say the rhyme *Grandma, what big eyes you've got* – use Class Cassette Unit 7, Part 5 | Round Up: the children say the rhyme – *Grandma, what big eyes you've got* – use Class Cassette Unit 7, Part 5 |

*Note:* The review Unit is Unit 3.

# Lesson 1
# Preparation Activities

## PREPARING YOUR LESSON

Prepare simple picture flash cards for:
*head, body, legs, tail, teeth, eyes, ears, nose, mouth, left hand, left foot, right hand, right foot, the tens up to 100 (10, 20–100).*

## WARM UP

Play *Chinese whispers* with numbers. Follow the same procedure as in Unit 1, Lesson 1. Whisper two numbers at a time.

## CHECK HOMEWORK

i. Show your completed pages for Unit 6. As in previous Units, ask the children what colour (grade) you deserve for your work. Turn to the *star chart* on the inside back cover of the book. Abide by the class decision on your grade, and colour in *star* 6 on the star chart.

ii. Ask the children to work in pairs. The children colour in their partner's *star* for this Unit. If there is any dispute, ask another child to be the final judge of grade.

iii. Check that parents have signed their children's Workpage.

## PRESENTING NEW LANGUAGE

The numbers: 10–100 (in tens). Use flash cards of the numbers as teaching aids.

a) Presentation.

i. Organise the class into a semi-circle. Give out the number flash cards (at random) to the children. You say the number as you give out the card. The children listen only.

ii. You say the numbers. The children hold up the appropriate flash card. They don't speak.

iii. You say the numbers. The children with the number flash cards hold them up. The remainder of the class show the value of the number with their fingers. They don't speak at this stage.

iv. Ask the children to put their number flash cards in various locations in the classroom. Organise the class into groups of three or four. Ask groups to stand near specific number flash cards. You then say the numbers. Groups must touch their toes when they hear their number. They don't speak.

v. Ask the children to move to another number of their choice. You say the first syllable of the number *(twen...; thir...)*, and point to a group. That group says the remainder *(-ty)*.
T: *Twen...*
G1: *...ty.*
T: *For...*
G2: *...ty...etc.*
Encourage the children to take your role. S1 says the *first syllable* of the number, and chooses a group to complete the number.

vi. Ask the children to stand in a circle. You choose one number flash card. You walk around the group with this number flash card and teach it to various children. You encourage all the children to do the same with the numbers they are holding.
T–S1: *Twenty.*
S1–T: *Fifty.*
T–S2: *Twenty.*
S2–T: *Seventy...etc.*
You move into the background as this activity gathers momentum. Encourage the children to help and correct each other.

vii. *Consolidation step:* You stop the activity. You say each of the numbers. The children listen only. The children then exchange flash cards and repeat the activity.

viii. Each child holds a number, or joins children who are holding a number. You ask the children to stand in a line, in numerical order. When they are in a line, encourage them to count off the numbers in numerical order, starting with ten. The children then exchange numbers, re-organise themselves into the correct numerical order and repeat the activity.

b) Practice.
Focus on the difference between *-teen* (stressed at the end – seven*teen*) and *-ty* (stressed at the beginning – *se*venty). Use Unit 7, Part 1 on the Class Cassette.

i. You play the Cassette. The children write the numbers they hear on paper, or with their fingers on their partner's back.

*Tapescript*
*Unit 7, Part 1. Listen and write down the numbers you hear.*
Number 1. 17, 17
Number 2. 40, 40
Number 3. 30, 30
Number 4. 19, 19

ii. Write up simple adding up and taking away sums on the board. For example:

15 + 17 = . . .   30 + 14 = . . .
20 + 16 = . . .   40 + 50 = . . .

Get the children to say and complete the sums.

iii. You dictate the sums to the children. The children write them down.
T: *Eighteen plus seventy equals . . . ?*

iv. Organise the children into pairs. The children dictate the sums to each other. You go round the class and help with the language if needed. As in previous Units, discourage the children from merely repeating after you. Give the children complete examples to listen to, leave the group, and allow them time to practise. Return later to check on results.

## GAME

Play *Simon says.*

i. Organise the class into pairs. Review the parts of the body that you are going to use in the game. Include:
*left hand, left foot, left arm, left leg, right hand, right foot, right arm, right leg, left ear, left eye, right ear, right eye.*
You give *pat your partner's . . .* or *touch your partner's . . . (gently)* instructions. Confirm the meaning of your instructions by working with S1 as your partner while you speak.
T: *Pat your partner's left arm. Touch your partner's right hand . . . etc.*

ii. Play *Simon says.*

*Rules*
The children must follow all instructions preceded by *Simon says.* However, if the instruction is not preceded by *Simon says* the children mustn't move. If they do move, they lose a team point, or are out of the game.

*Example Script*
*Simon says touch your right ear.*
*Simon says touch your right eye.*
*Simon says touch your left leg.*
*Simon says touch your right arm.*
*Touch your right ear.*

## ACTION GAME

* consolidating the use of numbers
* consolidating classroom language
* group formation activity

Use Unit 7, Part 2 on the Class Cassette. This is the first time the children have played this game, so follow Action Game Procedure 1 on page 15.

*Tapescript*
*Unit 7, Part 2. Listen and do the actions.*
Ready? Stand up please. Come here. Pick up three numbers. Say the whole number. Now put the numbers down.

## HOMEWORK

Ask the children to make cut-outs of their left and right hands. Explain and demonstrate the steps.

i. Draw round left and right hands with a pencil on a piece of paper.

ii. Cut round the outline with a pair of scissors.

iii. Colour in the 'cut-out' hands.

## ROUND UP

Making team numbers.
Divide the class into teams of six or seven children. Say a *-ty* or *-teen* number. The teams must show the *shape* of that number as a group with their bodies, or arms, or legs, etc. Allow the first team finished to leave the classroom first.

# Lesson 2
# Joining the Dots

## PREPARING YOUR LESSON

- Bring in pictures of real elephants.

- Find out facts and figures about elephants.

## WARM UP

Use the Action Game on the Class Cassette (Unit 7, Part 2). Follow Action Game Procedure 2 on page 18.

*Tapescript*
*Unit 7, Part 2. Listen and do the actions.*
Ready? Stand up please. Come here. Pick up three numbers. Say the whole number. Now put the numbers down.

## CHECK HOMEWORK

i.  Ask the children to show you the cut-out *hands* they have made. Ask them to put their initials on the backs of the hands.

ii. Collect the *hands*, mix them up, then ask the children to sort them into left and right. What's the difference?

iii. Make a display of the 'cut-outs' of the left and right hands. For example, display them biggest to smallest.

iv. Ask the children to guess which hand belongs to which student.

## ACTIVITY

Do the *Join the dots* activity. Use Unit 7, Part 3 on the Class Cassette.

i.  Play the Cassette. The children join up the dots.
*Note:* The numbers do NOT follow in ascending order.

*Tapescript*
*Unit 7, Part 3. Listen and join the dots.*
Find the number 6. Ready? Listen to the numbers. Join up the dots. 6 . . . 2 . . . 0 . . . 17 . . . 9 . . . 16 . . . 20 . . . 1 . . . 13 . . . 10 . . . 4 . . . 7 . . . 12 . . . 3 . . . 18 . . . 5 . . . 19 . . . 28 . . . 11 . . . 14 . . . 15.

Now find the number 38. Ready? Listen to the numbers. Join the dots. 38 . . . 35 . . . 45 . . . 47 . . . 37 . . . 48 . . . 30 . . . 50 . . . 31 . . . 33 . . . 56 . . . 42 . . . 40 . . . 34 . . . 32 . . . 49 . . . 39 . . . 43 . . . 46 . . . 44 . . . 41.

During the activity, stop the Cassette and ask the children to guess the next number, or say the last number:
T: *What was the last number, Sandi?*
S: *10.*
T: *What number is coming next, Simone?*
S: *7.*

ii. Get the children to colour in their pictures. They follow the instructions on the Cassette. Use Unit 7, Part 4 on the Class Cassette.

*Tapescript*     Elephant pic
*Unit 7, Part 4. Listen and colour your picture.*
1. Colour the left ear yellow.
2. Colour the right ear green.
3. Colour the trunk blue.
4. Colour the left legs pink.
5. Colour the right legs red.
6. Colour the tail brown.
7. Colour the head grey.

*Note:* The children can choose their own colour for the elephant's body.

## LANGUAGE PRACTICE

Encourage the children to ask and answer questions about their elephants.

i.  Review and consolidate *body parts* or *colours* vocabulary that you have noticed needs further work. If necessary, refer back to previous Units for the procedure for presenting new language.

ii. You ask the questions. The children give short, true answers.
T: *What colour's your elephant's left ear?*
S: *Yellow . . . etc.*

iii. Divide the class into two groups. You repeat your questions, leaving out key words. Group 1 helps supply the missing words from the questions. Select children from Group 2 to answer.
T: *What colour's your . . .*
G1: *Elephant's trunk?*
G2: *Blue.*
T: *What colour's . . .*
G1: *Your elephant's right ear?*
G2: *Green . . . etc.*

iv. Groups change roles and repeat this activity.

v. Choose S1. S1 comes to the front of the class. He or she points to parts of the elephant. Group 1 asks a *What colour . . . ?* question. Group 2 answers. Repeat this activity with a new S1.

vi. Organise the children into pairs. The children take turns to ask each other questions. You go round and help with the language. Then let them try. Encourage student-to-student correction rather than allowing the children merely to repeat line by line after you.

vii. Finally, show pictures of real elephants. Ask the children to guess facts about the elephants. Write the guesses on the board. Keep a note of these guesses. The children find out the real facts for homework. For example:
T: *How tall is this elephant, do you think?*
S: *300 (three, zero, zero) centimetres.*
T: *What do you think, Ana?*
S: *500 (five, zero, zero) centimetres.*
T: *And how high can it reach? . . . etc.*

## REVIEW

- reviewing and previewing how to describe animals
- practising *have/has*
- reviewing *body parts* vocabulary

Encourage the children to ask each other questions about beetles and mini-beasts.

i. Organise the children into a semi-circle. Ask them to turn back to Unit 3. Ask them questions about the beetles and mini-beasts they have drawn on page 7. They look at their drawings and give you true answers.

ii. Organise the children into groups of three or four.

iii. Choose a leader for each group. Ask a question, pause, then ask the question again, encouraging the leaders to ask the questions with you. Group members answer. Don't correct errors at this stage.
T: *How many legs does your beetle have?*
S: *Nine.*
T: *What colour's your beetle's head? . . . etc.*

iv. Change leaders. Repeat the activity without your prompts. You go round the class and help with the language if needed.

## HOMEWORK

Ask the children to find out facts and figures about elephants. Offer team points or mini-prizes for interesting facts and pictures.

## ROUND UP

Teach *Grandma, what big eyes you've got* using Unit 7, Part 5 on the Class Cassette.

*Tapescript*
Unit 7, Part 5. Listen and join in.
Grandma, what big eyes you've got.
   –All the better to see you with.
Grandma, what big ears you've got.
   –All the better to hear you with.
Grandma, what big hands you've got.
   –All the better to hold you with.
Grandma, what big teeth you've got.
   –All the better to eat you with.
HELP!

I see with my eyes
I hear with my ears
I hold things with my hands
I eat with my teeth

Tell little red riding hood
draw pics on board to illustrate
Retell story, point to pics. children
say word

# Lesson 3
# Follow Up Activities

## PREPARING YOUR LESSON

- Prepare your own Workpage, Student's Book page 15 for demonstration purposes.

- Bring in lots of coins of different sizes and values.

- Bring in pictures, facts and figures about elephants.

## WARM UP

Use the Action Game on the Class Cassette (Unit 7, Part 2). Follow Action Game Procedure 3 on page 20.

## CHECK HOMEWORK AND LANGUAGE PRACTICE

Get the children to show and say the information they have collected about elephants. Compare the facts with the guesses from the last lesson.
Encourage the children to talk about elephants.

i. You give examples. Point to the elephant as you speak.
T: *This is an elephant. It's three metres tall. It weighs 900 (nine, zero, zero) kilos. It eats leaves and grass and fruit.*

ii. You repeat your description, leaving out key words. The class says the missing words.
T: *This is . . .*
Ss: *An elephant*
T: *It's three . . .*
Ss: *Metres tall . . . etc.*

iii. S1 comes to the front of the class, points to an elephant and uses gestures to show what he or she wants the class to describe. The class gives the description. Repeat this activity with a new S1.

iv. Organise the children into groups of three or four. The children take turns to describe the elephants to their group. You go round and help with the language. Whenever feasible say a complete description while the children are listening. Then let them try.

v. Choose and encourage children to talk about elephants to the rest of the class. Allow errors. Don't correct the children as they speak.

## REVIEW

- consolidating numbers
- adding up money in English

The children add up the values of coins.

i. Draw three circles on the board to represent three coins.

ii. The children copy the three circles onto a sheet of paper.

iii. Put three coins in your hand. Don't show the children what the value of the coins is.

iv. The children guess the values of the coins in your hand and write the appropriate number values in their three circles.

v. Write up the total value of your coins on the board. Explain your addition in English.
T: *50p plus 10p plus 5p equals . . .*
S: *65p.*

vi. Organise the children into groups of three. The children take turns to add up the values of their circle coins in English to the rest of their group. You go round the class and help with the language.

## WORKPAGE

Complete the Workpage, Student's Book page 15. Use Unit 7, Parts A, B and C on the Home Cassette.

i. Demonstrate how to do Part A. Do the first example of the exercise in class with the children. Assign the rest for homework.

*Tapescript*
*Unit 7, Part A. Listen. Shade in the right numbers.*
Number 1. 17, 17
Number 2. 40, 40
Number 3. 30, 30
Number 4. 19, 19

ii. Review how to do Part B, the *Teach your parents* activity. Refer back to Unit 6, Lesson 3 for the procedure if necessary.

*Tapescript*
*Unit 7, Part B. Listen. Teach your parents.*
Ready? Stand up please. Come here. Pick up three numbers. Say the whole number. Now put the numbers down.

iii. Do Part C in class with the children. You play the Cassette, they complete the gaps, copying the words from the *cloud*.

*Tapescript*
*Unit 7, Part C. Listen again. Write in the missing words.*
Ready? Stand up please. Come here. Pick up three numbers. Say the whole number. Now put the numbers down.

iv. Demonstrate how to do Part D.

## HOMEWORK

i. Ask the children to complete page 15 of their *early bird* book.

ii. Encourage the children to ask their parents to sign their completed Workpage.

iii. Make sure the children bring in their Picture Dictionary for the next lesson.

## ROUND UP

Play *Grandma, what big eyes you've got* using the Class Cassette.
Divide the class into two teams. Team 1 says *grandma's* lines.
Team 2 says the remaining lines. Encourage the children to use lots of gestures and feeling when they speak. Allow extroverts to leave the classroom first.

*Tapescript*
*Unit 7, Part 5. Listen and join in.*
Grandma, what big eyes you've got.
 –All the better to see you with.
Grandma, what big ears you've got.
 –All the better to hear you with.
Grandma, what big hands you've got.
 –All the better to hold you with.
Grandma, what big teeth you've got.
 –All the better to eat you with.
HELP!

## EVALUATION

In terms of evaluation of this Unit, the following table can be used as a guide. You may photocopy and include it in your school record book. For simplicity, tick a column if you are satisfied with a child's performance; leave it blank if you are not happy.
*Note:* The table is a guide, and a record to refer back to. It is not intended as a grade list.

| Name | Activity completed | Can give the PR instructions for this Unit | Can understand your questions about elephants | Can give true responses | Can communicate information about elephants |
|---|---|---|---|---|---|
| | | | | | |
| | | | | | |
| | | | | | |
| | | | | | |
| | | | | | |
| | | | | | |

# Unit 8    Picture Dictionary Work

## INTRODUCTION

This is the second Dictionary Unit in the course. The aims are as follows:

- giving the children further practice of dictionary skill activities;

- encouraging the children to build their own, independent Picture Dictionary;

- consolidating awareness of an alphabetical filing system;

- giving further practice of spelling in English;

- reviewing and previewing vocabulary.

Table 1 (below) summarises the content of the Unit. Table 2 gives an outline of the key teaching steps.

Table 1

| The Children's Experience of Language Input across the Curriculum | | | Language Output from the Children in an Activity-Based Context | |
| --- | --- | --- | --- | --- |
| Activities and topics | Teacher's questions, instructions, and comments about: | Physical Response Activities | Vocabulary | Expressions and structures |
| Picture Dictionary | sorting and classifying words; using a dictionary | hop measure | art and craft family tape measure scissors eraser pencil glue numbers 100–1000 | in tens How tall . . . ? Can I have . . . ? Here you are. You're going to . . . (future) |

**Table 2**

| Lesson 1<br>Preparation Activities | Lesson 2<br>Main Activity:<br>Picture Dictionary Work | Lesson 3<br>Follow Up Activities |
|---|---|---|
| Warm Up: play *Scissors, stone, paper* | Warm Up: Action Game: use Class Cassette Unit 8, Part 2 (follow Procedure 2) | Warm Up: Action Game: use Class Cassette Unit 8, Part 2 (follow Procedure 3) |
| Check Homework: colour in *star 7*; review the children's Picture Dictionaries | Check Homework: play with new Snapdragon | Check Homework and Language Practice: the children use their own own Picture Dictionaries |
| Presenting New Language: using numbers 100–1000 – use Class Cassette Unit 8, Part 1; recognition of spellings | Main Activity: the children sort and file the items on Unit 8 Activity Page (Student's Book page 35); cut out items on page 37 | Unit 8 Workpage (Student's Book page 17): use Home Cassette Unit 8, Parts B and C |
| Action Game: use Class Cassette Unit 8, Part 2 (follow Procedure 1) | Language Practice: requests – use Class Cassette Unit 8, Part 3 | Review: use Class Cassette Unit 8, Part 4; role play |
| Review: Unit 5 – the children play with their Snapdragons | Game: play *Bingo* with vocabulary items from Unit 8 | Game or Song: free choice |
| Homework: make another Snapdragon | Homework: the children file the items from page 37 into their own Picture Dictionaries | Homework: finish off Workpage (Student's Book page 17) |
| Round Up: the children sing *One finger, one thumb, keep moving* – use Class Cassette Unit 5, Part 3 | Round Up: play *Scissors, stone, paper* | Round Up: play story game with *family* and *classroom items* as key words |

*Note:* The review Unit is Unit 5.

# Lesson 1
# Preparation Activities

## PREPARING YOUR LESSON

– Prepare flash cards for numbers 100–1000 (in hundreds).

– Prepare picture flash cards or real items for the vocabulary on page 35 of the Student's Book.

– Prepare *word* flash cards for the vocabulary.

– Read through the Introduction and teaching notes for Unit 4.

## WARM UP

Play *Scissors, stone, paper*. The class plays the game in pairs:
S1 + S2: *Scissors, stone, paper!*
Refer back to the Round Up stage of Unit 4, Lesson 2 for the procedure.

## CHECK HOMEWORK

a) Grading Unit 7.

i. Show your completed pages for Unit 7. As in previous Units, ask the children what colour (grade) you deserve for your work. Turn to the *star chart* on the inside back cover of the book. Abide by the class decision on your grade, and colour in *star 7* on the star chart.

ii. Ask the children to work in pairs. The children colour in their partner's *star* for this Unit. If there is any dispute, ask another child to be the final judge of grade.

iii. Check that parents have signed their children's Workpage.

b) Discussing the Picture Dictionaries.

i. Ask the children to show you their Picture Dictionaries.

ii. Organise the children into pairs or threes. Ask them to look at each other's Dictionaries. This is a free stage. Allow the children about five minutes to exchange ideas and views.

iii. Make sure that any children who have forgotten their Dictionaries, bring them for the next lesson.

## PRESENTING NEW LANGUAGE

- reviewing vocabulary
- practising spelling of the vocabulary from this Unit

a) Review the numbers 10–100. Use Unit 8, Part 1 on the Class Cassette.

i. Organise the children into a semi-circle. Ask various children to count in tens.
T: *Marco. Count from 10 to 90 in tens.*
S: *Ten, twenty, thirty, forty . . . etc.*

ii. Organise the children into groups of three or four. Play the Class Cassette (Unit 8, Part 1).

iii. Choose a leader for each group. Play the Cassette. Pause the Cassette after each instruction, rewind and play the instruction again, encouraging the leaders to give the instructions with the Cassette. Group members *count*. Don't correct errors at this stage.

*Tapescript*
*Unit 8, Part 1. Listen and count in tens.*
1. Count to 50, in tens.
2. Count from 20 to 70, in tens.
3. Count from 40 to 100, in tens.
4. Count from 30 to 90, in tens.

iv. Change leaders. Repeat the activity without the Cassette. You go round the class and help with the language if needed. As before, don't encourage the children merely to repeat after you. Give the children complete examples to listen to, leave the group, and allow them time to practise. Return later to check on results.

b) Introduce the numbers 100–1000 (in hundreds) using number flash cards. Follow the usual procedure for presenting new language. Refer back to Units 1–4 if necessary. Encourage the children to dictate numbers to you, and to each other.

c) Review the vocabulary on page 35 of the Student's Book using your flash cards and real items.

i. Show and name the items or flash cards. The children watch and listen only.

ii. Ask the children to *pick up and give* items to other children.
T: *Rikki. Pick up the glue. Give it to Yoshiko . . . etc.*

iii. Ask the children to identify the items they are holding. Use gesture to help explain your meaning.
T: *Who has the scissors? Me or you?*
S: *Me.*
T: *Elsie. Who has the tape measure?*
S: *Toni . . . etc.*

iv. Ask the children to stand in a circle. You choose one flash card or item. You walk around the group with this flash card and teach it to various children. You encourage all the children to do the same with the flash cards or items they are holding. Move into the background as this activity gathers momentum. Encourage the children to help and correct each other.

v. *Consolidation step:* You stop the activity. You name each of the items. The children hold their item or flash card above their heads when they hear their word. The children then exchange flash cards and items, and repeat the above activity.

d) Focus on spelling[1].

Organise the class into two teams. The teams stand or sit in a large semi-circle. Collect in all the picture flash cards (and items) and lay them face down on the floor or desks. Display the *word* flash cards, word upwards, on the floor or desks. The children from each team take turns to compete against each other in a variety of mini-challenges. For example:

i. You name a vocabulary item. The first child to touch the word for that item scores a team point – if he or she can then match the spelling to the real item or picture of the item.

ii. You start to spell a word. The first child to guess the word you are spelling scores a team point.

iii. You ask the two competing children to close their eyes. Ask them how to spell one word each. Correct spelling scores a point.
T: *How do you spell crayon? . . . etc.*

iv. Ask S1 to take your role. He or she asks the spelling questions. Don't correct while S1 is speaking. If there are errors, when a child has finished, and before asking a new student to be the teacher, you have another turn. In this way you give the class another chance to listen to a correct example.

v. Finally, organise the children into pairs. The children turn to page 35. S1 asks a spelling question. S2 spells the word without looking at the page:
S1: *How do you spell paper?*
S2: *p. . .a. . .p. . .e. . .r . . . etc.*

## ACTION GAME

i. Use Unit 8, Part 2 on the Class Cassette. This is the first time the children have played this game so follow Action Game Procedure 1 on page 15.

*Tapescript*
*Unit 8, Part 2. Listen and do the actions.*
You're going to hop. Ready? 1 . . . 2 . . . 3 . . . hop. Now, pick up a tape measure. Measure the distance. How far did you hop?

ii. Play a team game. Organise the class into two teams. Choose a team leader for each team. Pairs from each team hop against each other.
Help the team leaders to ask *How far did you hop?* after each hop.
S1: *How far did you hop?*
S2: *One hundred and thirty five centimetres.*
Change team leaders after two hops.

## REVIEW

Review Unit 5. Ask the children to turn back to Unit 5, pages 10 and 11, in their *early bird* books.

i. Review how to play the game. Play with S1. Review the language as you play the game. For example:
T: *Pick a number.*
S: *5.*
T: *1. . .2. . .3. . .4. . .5. Pick another number.*
S: *2.*
T: *1. . .2. Pick a colour.*
S: *Blue.*
T: *b. . .l. . .u. . .e. Pick another colour.*
S: *Green.*
T: *g. . .r. . .e. . .e. . .n. Now pick a number.*
S: *7.*
T: *You get a . . . hot dog. Here you are . . .*

ii. Pairwork. Organise the class into pairs. Pairs play with their Snapdragons. You go round the class and help with the language if needed.

## HOMEWORK

Ask the children to make a new Snapdragon using the numbers and items from page 35 instead of colours and fast foods. Ask them to bring their new Snapdragons to the next lesson.

## ROUND UP

Review the song *One finger, one thumb, keep moving.* Use Unit 5, Part 3 on the Class Cassette for reference if necessary.

---

[1] Spelling may be inappropriate for younger children, in which case omit this activity for the time being.

# Lesson 2
# Picture Dictionary Work

## PREPARING YOUR LESSON

- Prepare large simple flash cards for the new headings on page 16: *art and craft, family, measuring*. One method is to make enlarged photocopies of the headings, and glue them onto thin card.

- Bring in the flash cards and real items that you used last lesson.

- Bring in your flash cards (from Unit 4) for the *action* and *numbers* headings.

- Bring in photocopies of page 37 as spares for any children who would like to file items under different headings.

## WARM UP

Use the Action Game on the Class Cassette (Unit 8, Part 2). Follow Action Game Procedure 2 on page 18.

*Tapescript*
*Unit 8, Part 2. Listen and do the actions.*
You're going to hop. Ready? 1 . . . 2 . . . 3 . . . hop.
Now pick up a tape measure. Measure the distance.
How far did you hop?

Jumping

## CHECK HOMEWORK

Ask the children to show you their Snapdragons. Organise the class into pairs. Pairs play *Snapdragon.* You go round and offer advice on language where necessary. Treat this activity as a free stage.

## ACTIVITY

Dictionary work with the items on page 35 of the Student's Book.

a) Teach the three new Picture Dictionary Headings (*art and craft, family, measuring*) on page 16. Review the *numbers* and *action* headings.

  i. Organise the class into a large semi-circle.

  ii. You show and name each *heading* flash card. The children watch and listen only.

  iii. Display the headings on the board or wall. Ask the children to point to the various headings. The children don't speak at this stage.

  iv. Ask the children to stand under the headings.
  T: *Jeanne, stand under the family heading. Marianne, stand under the measuring heading . . . etc.*

  v. Ask the children to identify the headings:
  T: *Who's standing under the art and craft heading? Hands up. What heading is Maria standing under, Pepi?*
  S: *Numbers . . . etc.*

b) Cutting out the items.

  i. Organise the class into groups of four. The children sit in their groups. Choose a *tidy monitor* for each group.

  ii. Check that all groups have access to a pair of scissors.

  iii. Ask the children to turn to pages 35 and 37 in their *early bird* books. Point out the differences between pages 35 and 37.

  iv. Give instructions to cut out items from page 35.
  T: *Does everybody have a pair of scissors? Everyone hold up your scissors. Now, cut out the tape measure. Only the tape measure. . . What picture are we going to cut out next? Kilos or paper or grandad?*
  S: *Grandad.*
  T: *Hands up if you think we're going to cut out grandad next. Well this time you're wrong. We're going to cut out paper. Everybody cut out paper . . . etc.*

  v. Give these types of instructions for four items, then ask the children to continue cutting out the rest of the items by themselves. Go round the class while the children are working. Ask *going to* questions:
  T: *What picture are you going to cut out next? Are you going to cut out the crayon or the glue?* Encourage the children to ask each other similar questions while they are working. Discourage the children from merely repeating after you. Give the children the complete examples to listen to, leave the group, and allow them time to practise. Return later to check on results.

  vi. Ask the children to cut up page 37. They put these items in their *bits and pieces* envelopes. When they have finished, organise the class into a semi-circle.

c) Sorting and filing the items from page 35 onto page 16 of the *early bird* book.

  i. Put your flash cards of the headings on the board.

ii. Show the flash cards for the vocabulary items. Ask the children to put the flash cards of the vocabulary items under the correct headings.
T: *What's this Miki?*
S: *A tape measure.*
T: *Where does the tape measure go? Which heading? Measuring or numbers or family or . . . ? Where does it go? Show me.*
S: *Here . . . etc.*
Note: Encourage the children to suggest more than one *filing* alternative. For example: *tape measure* could reasonably be filed under *measuring, art and craft* and possibly *numbers*. If the children wish to do this, hand out your extra photocopies of the items.

iii. The class work in their groups and sort all their items from page 35 under the headings printed on page 16. You go round and ask questions about the vocabulary and the classification of the items.
T: *What's this called in English?*
S: *A crayon.*
T: *Which heading does it go under?*
S: *Art and craft . . . etc.*

## LANGUAGE PRACTICE

• practising classroom requests

i. Organise the class into pairs. The children take out their dictionary items from their *bits and pieces* envelopes.

ii. Play Unit 8, Part 3 on the Class Cassette. Stop the Cassette after each question. Ask the children to give you the correct picture.

*Tapescript*
*Unit 8, Part 3. Listen and give your friend the right pictures.*
1. Can I have the ruler, please?
2. Can I have the eraser, please?
3. Can I have the pencil, please?
4. Can I have the tape measure, please?
5. Can I have the scissors, please?
6. Can I have the glue, please?
7. Can I have the scales, please?
8. Can I have the felt tip, please?

iii. Choose S1. Replay the Cassette. S1 gives the requests with the Cassette. You give S1 the correct pictures, and a short response.
S1: *Can I have the glue, please?*
T: *Here you are.*

iv. Change S1. Repeat the activity. This time S1 chooses children to respond to the request.

v. Pairwork. Repeat the activity with the Cassette. You go round the class and help with the language if needed. As before, don't encourage the children merely to repeat after you. Give the children complete examples to listen to, leave the group, and allow them time to practise. Return later to check on results.

vi. The children return their items to the *bits and pieces* envelope at the end of the activity.

## GAME

• reviewing vocabulary
• focusing on listening skills

Play *Bingo* with the vocabulary items on page 37.

i. Ask the children to take out any three items from their *bits and pieces* envelopes.

ii. You put all your pictures from page 37 into a bag or box. When the children are ready, you pick out the pictures one at a time from the bag, and call them out. The first child to match his or her three items wins a prize (e.g. a sweet), and becomes the caller for a repeat game.

## HOMEWORK

i. Ask the children to glue the items from page 37 (now in their *bits and pieces* envelopes) into their Picture Dictionaries under the appropriate headings.

ii. Ask the children to draw (or find a cut-out from a magazine) one additional item for their *numbers, art and craft, measuring,* and *family* pages.

## ROUND UP

Play *Scissors, stone, paper.* Refer back to Unit 4, Lesson 2 for the procedure.

# Lesson 3
# Follow Up Activities

## PREPARING YOUR LESSON

Prepare your Workpage, Student's Book page 17 for demonstration purposes.

## WARM UP

Use the Action Game on the Class Cassette (Unit 8, Part 2). Follow Action Game Procedure 3 on page 20.

## CHECK HOMEWORK AND LANGUAGE PRACTICE

a) Check the children have filed the items correctly in their new Dictionaries.

b) Ask the children to talk about the pages in their Picture Dictionary.

   i. You give the example. Point to your *art and craft* page as you speak:
   T: *This is my art and craft page. This is a picture of a pencil. This is a picture of a crayon . . . etc.*

   ii. You repeat your description, leaving out key words. The class says the missing words.
   T: *This is my . . .*
   Ss: *Art and craft page . . .*
   T: *This is a picture . . .*
   Ss: *Of a crayon . . . etc.*

   iii. S1 comes to the front of the class. S1 points to items on his or her *art and craft* page. The class describes them. Repeat this activity with a new S1 and a different Dictionary page.

   iv. Organise the children into groups of three or four. The children take turns to describe the content of pages in their new Dictionaries to their group. (Also encourage them to check each other's spellings.) You go round and help with the language. Whenever feasible say a complete description while the children are listening. Then let them try. Encourage student-to-student correction rather than allowing the children merely to repeat line by line after you. Choose and encourage the children to talk about their Picture Dictionary pages to the rest of the class. Allow errors. Don't correct the children as they speak.

## WORKPAGE

- recording work done in this Unit
- reviewing and consolidating

Complete the Workpage, Student's Book page 17. Use Unit 8, Parts B and C on the Home Cassette.

   i. Demonstrate how to do Part A. The children must complete the missing information and colour in where appropriate. Do the first two examples in class, and assign the remainder for homework.

   ii. Demonstrate how to do Part B. Use Unit 8, Part B on the Home Cassette. Show your own page 17.

   iii. When the children understand what to do, organise the class into pairs.

   iv. You play the Cassette. Pause the Cassette after each instruction, rewind and play the instruction again, encouraging S1 in each pair to speak with the Cassette. S2 counts the appropriate numbers.

   v. The children change roles, then partners and repeat the activity. You go round the class helping where necessary. Finally, the children circle the correct numbers in each example.

*Tapescript*
*Unit 8, Part B. Listen. Count in tens. Circle the numbers you've counted.*
1. Count to 50, in tens.
2. Count from 20 to 70, in tens.
3. Count from 40 to 100, in tens.
4. Count from 30 to 90, in tens.

   vi. Review how to do Part C, the *Teach your parents* activity[2]. Use Unit 8, Part C on the Home Cassette. Follow a similar procedure to the one used in Unit 2. Do a role play for the *Teach your parents* situation. Choose two children. S1 is the parent. S2 is him- or herself.

*Tapescript*
*Unit 8, Part C. Listen. Teach your parents.*
You're going to hop. Ready? 1 . . . 2 . . . 3 . . . hop. Now, pick up a tape measure. Measure the distance. How far did you hop?

## REVIEW

- consolidating family vocabulary
- using prepositions of location
- giving classroom instructions in English
- role play

---

[2] This activity may be too difficult for younger children. With a younger class, you will need to do a higher percentage of the Workpage activities in class time.

Use Unit 8, Part 4 on the Class Cassette.

i. Assign the *family roles* to the children: *mum, dad, grandma, grandad, Pete* and *Julie*. The remaining children are observers.

*Tapescript*
*Unit 8, Part 4. Listen. Tell your family where to stand. Then take their photo.*
Mum, dad, grandma and grandad, stand over there. Pete, stand in front of mum. Julie, stand in front of grandad. Grandad, stand next to mum. Now smile. Say cheese. Thank you.

ii. You take the role of *photographer*. Play the Cassette. Use lots of gestures to position the family.

iii. You repeat the instructions, leaving out key words. The observing group says the missing words.
T: *Mum, dad, grandma and* . . .
Ss: *Grandad.*
T: *Stand* . . .
Ss: *Over there . . . etc.*

iv. S1 comes to the front of the class. S1 uses gestures (but doesn't speak) to position the family. The remaining *observers* give the instructions.

v. The groups change roles. The observers take the *family* roles and vice versa. Repeat the activity with a new S1.

vi. Organise the children into groups of four. The children decide on the *family roles* within their groups. They take turns to be *photographer* and act out the *photo-taking* role play. You go round and help with the language.

vii. Choose and encourage groups to perform their role play to the rest of the class. Allow errors. Don't correct the children as they speak. Encourage all attempts.

## GAME OR SONG

Free choice. Ask the children if they want to play a game, or sing. Suggest *Snapdragon,* or one of the songs or rhymes learnt so far.

## HOMEWORK

Ask the children to complete page 17 of their *early bird* book. Encourage the children to ask their parents to sign their completed Workpage.

## ROUND UP

Play a story game. Use *classroom items* and *family members* as the key words. Use a similar procedure to the story game stage in Unit 3, Lesson 2.

*Example Story Script*
*One day last week I went to my* **grandma's** *house with my* **sister**. *It was raining. I was bored, so my* **grandad** *gave me a* **pencil** *and some* **paper**. **Grandad** *gave my* **sister** *some coloured* **paper** *and some* **glue**. *I drew a picture of my* **mum** . . . *etc.*

## EVALUATION

In terms of evaluation of this Unit, the following table can be used as a guide. You may photocopy and include it in your school record book. For simplicity, tick a column if you are satisfied with a child's performance; leave it blank if you are not happy. *Note:* The table is a guide, and a record to refer back to. It is not intended as a grade list.

| Name | Has sorted and classified items successfully | Is building up own Picture Dictionary | Can understand your questions about dictionary items | Can give true responses | Can communicate information about own Dictionary pages |
|---|---|---|---|---|---|
| | | | | | |
| | | | | | |
| | | | | | |
| | | | | | |

# Unit 9   Making a Favourites Crest

## INTRODUCTION

This Unit reviews language learned so far, and extends the children's knowledge in English of *foods, drinks, colours and toys*. The content of the Unit focuses on making a *favourites crest*. The children either draw on this crest, or find pictures, cut-outs and labels to stick on, to represent their favourite items.

The co-operative nature of the main activity is important in strengthening relationships between the children. This in turn will encourage student-to-student help and support in the language areas of the Unit.

Through the practical activities in Unit 9, the children will:

- work together and make a *favourites crest;*

- talk about their *favourite* items in English;

- state *likes and dislikes;*

- ask each other questions about favourites, likes and dislikes;

- consolidate their active recognition of a wide range of question forms in English.

Table 1 (below) summarises the content of the Unit. Table 2 gives an outline of the key teaching steps.

Table 1

| | | | | |
|---|---|---|---|---|
| The Children's Experience of Language Input across the Curriculum | | | Language Output from the Children in an Activity-Based Context | |
| Activities and topics | Teacher's questions, instructions, and comments about: | Physical Response Activities | Vocabulary | Expressions and structures |
| making a *favourites crest* | likes and dislikes; favourites; using charts to record information | hold open lick swallow | favourite toy/game *foods* *drinks* | I do/don't my favourite . . .    is . . . me too<br><br>How many . . . How much . . . Do- questions<br><br>I like/don't like . . . |

**Table 2**

| Lesson 1<br>**Preparation Activities** | Lesson 2<br>**Main Activity:**<br>**Making a Favourites Crest** | Lesson 3<br>**Follow Up Activities** |
|---|---|---|
| Warm Up: play *Chinese whispers* with foods | Warm Up: Action Game: use Class Cassette Unit 9, Part 1 (follow Procedure 2) | Warm Up: Action Game: use Class Cassette Unit 9, Part 1 (follow Procedure 3) |
| Check Homework: Picture Dictionaries; colour in *star 8* | Check Homework: display and sort favourite items | Check Homework: check Unit 9 Activity Page (Student's Book page 18) |
| Presenting New Language: the children's favourite items | Activity: the children make group *favourites crests* | Language Practice: describe the group *favourites crests*; answer the questions on Class Cassette Unit 9, Part 3 |
| Action Game: use Class Cassette Unit 9, Part 1 (follow Procedure 1) | Language Practice: *What's your favourite . . . ?* use Class Cassette Unit 9, Part 2 | Unit 9 Workpage (Student's Book page 19): use Home Cassette Unit 9, Parts A, B, C and D |
| Review: Unit 6 – story lines | Homework: make individual *favourites crests* on Unit 9 Activity Page (Student's Book page 18) | Game or song: free choice |
| Homework: bring in favourite items | Round Up: tidy up the classroom | Homework: finish off Workpage (Student's Book page 19) |
| Round Up: the children say the rhyme *Grandma, what big eyes you've got* – use Class Cassette Unit 7, Part 5 | | Round Up: the children skip to the rhyme *I like coffee, I like tea* – use Class Cassette Unit 9, Part 4 |

*Note:* The review Unit is Unit 6.

# Lesson 1
# Preparation Activities

## PREPARING YOUR LESSON

– Prepare flash cards and real items for your favourite things and people.

– Bring in a large (poster size) sheet of thick paper or thin card.

## WARM UP

• developing observational skills
• group formation
• using mime and gesture

Play *Chinese mimes* with foods.

i. Organise the class into two team lines. You stand at the back of the lines. The lines face the board, and must not look at you.

ii. You touch the shoulders of the last children (S1 and S2) in each line. S1 and S2 turn round to face you.

iii. You do a short *mime* for a food with your hands and arms. For example: the outline of a fish. Only S1 and S2 are allowed to see your mime.

iv. S1 and S2 touch the shoulders of the next children in their team lines (S3 and S4). S3 and S4 turn round to face S1 and S2. The remaining children in the teams must not see what is happening.

v. S1 and S2 pass on your mime to their team members (S3 and S4).

vi. The children continue to pass on your mime down the team lines. The children at the front of the line do the mime for the whole class. What do the front two children think it is? How much has it changed?

## CHECK HOMEWORK

i. Show your completed pages for Unit 8, and your Picture Dictionary. As for previous Units, ask the children what colour (grade) you deserve for your work. Turn to the *star chart* on the inside back cover of *early bird*. Abide by the class decision on your grade, and colour in *star 8* on the star chart.

ii. Ask the children to work in pairs. The children colour in their partner's *star* for this Unit. If there is any dispute, ask another child to be the final judge of grade.

iii. Check that parents have signed their children's Workpage.

## PRESENTING NEW LANGUAGE

a) Find out the children's favourites. Use flash cards, drawings and real items as teaching aids.

i. Say the names of popular foods, drinks, colours and toys. Give out your flash cards to the children as you say the names of the items. The children listen.

ii. Ask the children to pick up and give items or flash cards to other children.
T: *Rikki. Pick up the chocolate ice-cream. Give it to Yoshiko . . . etc.*

iii. Ask the children to identify the items they are holding. Use gestures to help explain your meaning.
T: *Who has the bicycle? Me or you?*
S: *Me.*
T: *Eva. Who has the coke? . . . etc.*

iv. Encourage the children to name their own favourites. For example:
T: *What's this, Christina?*
S: *An ice-cream.*
T: *Hands up if you like ice-cream. What's your favourite ice-cream, Jon?*
S: *Chocolate.*
T: *Hands up if your favourite ice-cream is chocolate ice-cream. Hands up if your favourite ice-cream is strawberry. What's your favourite ice-cream, Yoko?*
S: *Tutti Frutti . . . etc.*

b) Record class favourites on a simple chart.

i. Draw simple headings for *colours, toys and games, food and drink* on your large sheet of paper or card. Draw columns under the headings. Display this chart on the board.

ii. Organise the class into groups of four. Appoint a leader (S1) for each group.

iii. Give each group four blank sheets of A4 size paper. Each group copies your headings onto their blank sheets of paper: one heading per sheet.

iv. The children draw their favourites onto these sheets of paper. When finished, the group leaders come to the board and record (draw) their group's results on your class chart.

c) Feedback on the results.

i. Ask the children to tell you the class's favourite, second favourite, and third favourite items under each category.
T: *What's the favourite food?*
S: *Chocolate mint ice-cream.*
T: *How many children chose hamburgers? Three or four?*
S: *Three . . . etc.*
Keep this chart for reference purposes.

## ACTION GAME

Use Unit 9, Part 1 on the Class Cassette. Follow Action Game Procedure 1 on page 15.

*Favourite food drink ice-cream toy.*

*Tapescript*
*Unit 9, Part 1. Listen and do the actions.*
Ready? Hold an ice-cream in your right hand. Open your mouth. Lick the ice-cream. Swallow. Lick your lips. Yum.

## REVIEW

Review Unit 6. Ask the children to turn back to pages 12 and 13 in their *early bird* books. Can they remember the story lines? Play Unit 6, Part 2 on the Class Cassette.

i. Organise the class into a semi-circle. Ask them to turn to page 12 in their *early bird* books.

ii. Say the story lines below at random. Ask the children to say the corresponding number on the cartoon pictures.

iii. Organise the children into groups of three or four. Choose a leader for each group. Play the Cassette (Unit 6, Part 2). The children point to the correct pictures.

*Tapescript*
*Unit 6, Part 2. Listen and hold up the right pictures.*
1. This is Andy.
2. This is Andy again.
3. This is a hamburger.
4. This is another hamburger.
5. These are french fries.
6. These are more french fries.
7. Andy asks for a yummy hamburger.
8. This is the ketchup.
9. Andy puts lots of ketchup on the hamburger.
10. This is Annie.
11. This is Annie again.
12. Annie says 'Hi' to Andy. Andy jumps.
13. Oh no! The ketchup goes all over the man.

iv. Play the Cassette again. Pause the Cassette after each story line, rewind and play the story line again, encouraging the leaders to say the story lines with the Cassette. Group members say the corresponding number on the cartoon pictures. Don't correct errors at this stage.

v. Change leaders. Repeat the activity, without the Cassette. You go round the class and help with the language if needed.

## HOMEWORK

Ask the children to find and bring in their *favourite* items for the next lesson. The children can bring in the *real* things, or cut-outs, or labels, or drawings to represent their favourites. Show and pass round examples of your own favourites.

## ROUND UP

Review the rhyme from Unit 7 on the Class Cassette: *Grandma, what big eyes you've got.* Refer back to Unit 7, Lesson 3 for the procedure.

# Lesson 2
# Making a Favourites Crest

## PREPARING YOUR LESSON

– Prepare large (poster size) sheets of thin card or thick paper. If blank materials are not available, use the backs of old posters.

– Prepare a large blank crest for demonstration purposes.

– Complete your own Student's Book page 18. Use drawings for your favourites.

– Bring in spare *favourite* labels, cut-outs, etc. of typical children's favourite foods, drinks, toys and games.

## WARM UP

Use the Action Game on the Class Cassette (Unit 9, Part 1). Follow Action Game Procedure 2 on page 18.

*Tapescript*
*Unit 9, Part 1. Listen and do the actions.*
Ready? Hold an ice-cream in your right hand. Open your mouth. Lick the ice-cream. Swallow. Lick your lips. Yum.

## CHECK HOMEWORK

Sort and display the items, labels and cut-outs that the children have brought in.

i.   You name and identify the most common items. The children watch and listen.

ii.  S1 comes to the front of the class and points to the items. You identify them.

iii. Repeat this activity with a new S1. This time the class identifies the items.

iv. Organise the children into groups of three or four. The children take turns to describe their favourites to their group. You go round and help with the language.

## ACTIVITY

The children make large *favourites crests*. You can display these crests at the end of the activity.

i.   Demonstrate and explain what you want the children to do. Make all necessary materials (scissors, glue, large sheets of paper or card, extra items) available on a central table or on the desks.

ii.  Divide the class into groups of four or five. Appoint a group leader who also acts as a *tidy monitor*. Explain and demonstrate the aims of the activity: to make a giant *favourites crest*. Explain that all the children must take part. The crest must be the result of cutting and gluing as well as drawing. Groups discuss the materials they need (mother tongue). Group leaders collect the materials from the materials table.

iii. You go round and chat to the groups in English while they are working. Ask them questions, make comments, using lots of gestures to help explain your meaning. For example:
T: *What's your favourite food, Lidia?*
S: *Chocolate ice-cream.*
T: *How about you, Henri?*
S: *Me too.*
T: *Whose favourite is this?*
S: *My favourite.*
T: *Does anyone else like computer games? . . . etc.*
In addition, where feasible, help individual children with any additional vocabulary they may want.

*Note:* The main aim of this stage of the activity is for the children to make the crest. To do this, they need to co-operate as a group. This co-operation is, in itself, an extremely important learning experience. At this stage of the course, the children do not have the language to discuss and chat in English. They will therefore chat in their mother tongue, introducing occasional English words. This is quite acceptable, since the other main purpose of this activity is to involve the children in the creation of a language text: once the crests are completed, you will be using them as student generated language texts.
However, encourage the children to ask for what they want in English, teaching the common classroom expressions and phrases as they naturally occur within the activity. For example: *Can I have a pencil? I don't have any glue. Can I borrow your scissors? etc.*

iv. Stop the activity at least ten minutes before the end of the lesson. Collect in and store the crests.

## LANGUAGE PRACTICE

Use Unit 9, Part 2 on the Class Cassette.

i.  Organise the children into a semi-circle. Ask them the questions or play the Cassette.

    *Tapescript*
    *Unit 9, Part 2.* *Listen and give true answers.*
    1. What's your favourite food?
    2. What's your favourite drink?
    3. What's your favourite ice-cream?
    4. What's your favourite toy?

ii. Organise the children into groups of three or four. Choose a leader for each group. Play the Cassette again. This time, pause the Cassette after each question, rewind and play the question again, encouraging the leaders to ask the questions with the Cassette. Group members answer. Don't correct errors at this stage.

iii. Change leaders. Repeat the activity, without the Cassette. You go round the class and help with the language if needed.

## HOMEWORK

Ask the children to make individual *favourites crests* on page 18 of their *early bird* books. Allow the children two homeworks to do this. Demonstrate and explain this activity using your own completed page 18. Since space is limited on this crest, ask the children to draw their favourites onto page 18, or stick on very small cut-outs.

## ROUND UP

Tidy up the classroom. Challenge the children to have the cleanest and tidiest work areas. Allow the tidiest to leave the classroom first.

D

# Lesson 3
# Follow Up Activities

## PREPARING YOUR LESSON

– Prepare your own Workpage, Student's Book page 19 for demonstration purposes.

– Bring in a skipping rope.

## WARM UP

Use the Action Game on the Class Cassette (Unit 9, Part 1). Follow Action Game Procedure 3 on page 20.

## CHECK HOMEWORK

Ask the children to show you how they are getting on with their individual *favourites crests* on page 18 of their *early bird* books. Ask a range of general questions. Hold up and praise the children's work.
T: *Whose is this crest?*
S: *Toni's.*
T: *What's Toni's favourite drink?*
S: *Coke.*
T: *Whose favourites are Madonna and chocolate ice-cream? . . . etc.*

## LANGUAGE PRACTICE

Encourage the children to talk about their group *favourites crests*.

i. Organise the children into their groups from last lesson. Give out the group crests.

ii. Join one group and describe the crest. Point to the *favourites* as you speak.
T: *This is our favourites crest. Our favourite foods are chocolate cake and hot dogs. Our favourite colours are yellow and red. Our favourite drinks are coke and lemonade.*

iii. You repeat your description, leaving out key words. The class says the missing words.
T: *This is our . . .*
Ss: *Favourites crest.*
T: *Our favourite foods . . .*
Ss: *Are chocolate cake . . . etc.*

iv. Group 1 comes to the front of the class. They hold up their crest and point to their favourite items. The class describes them. Repeat this activity with a new group.

v. Organise the children into new groups of four. The children take turns to describe their crests to their new group. You go round and help with the language.

vi. Use Unit 9, Part 3 on the Class Cassette. Organise the children into groups of three or four. Choose a leader for each group. Play the Cassette.

*Tapescript*
*Unit 9, Part 3. Listen and give true answers.*
1. Do you like chocolate ice-cream?
2. Do you like chocolate cake?
3. Do you like coke?
4. Do you like ketchup?

vii. Play the Cassette again. This time, pause the Cassette after each question, rewind and play the question again, encouraging the leaders to ask the questions with the Cassette. Group members answer. Don't correct errors at this stage.

viii. Change leaders. Repeat the activity, without the Cassette. As in previous Units, you go round the class and help with the language if needed. Encourage the children to introduce questions of their own.

## WORKPAGE

The children complete the Workpage, Student's Book page 19. Use Unit 9, Parts A, B, C and D on the Home Cassette. Explain and demonstrate what to do, then assign the exercises for homework[1].

*Tapescript*
*Unit 9, Part A. Listen. Draw your answers. Write in the words. Colour your drawings.*
1. What's your favourite food?
2. What's your favourite drink?
3. What's your favourite ice-cream?
4. What's your favourite toy?

*Unit 9, Part B. Listen, draw and write yes or no.*
1. Do you like chocolate ice-cream?
2. Do you like chocolate cake?
3. Do you like coke?
4. Do you like ketchup?

*Unit 9, Part C. Listen. Teach your parents.*
Ready? Hold an ice-cream in your right hand. Open your mouth. Lick the ice-cream. Swallow. Lick your lips. Yum.

---

[1] This activity may be too difficult for younger children. With a younger class, you will need to do a higher percentage of the Workpage activities in class time.

*Unit 9, Part D. Listen again. Look. Write in the missing words.*
Ready? Hold an ice-cream in your right hand. Open your mouth. Lick the ice-cream. Swallow. Lick your lips. Yum.

## GAME OR SONG

Free choice. Ask the children if they want to play a game, or sing. Suggest *Mirror statues* (from Unit 6, Lesson 1), or one of the songs or rhymes learnt so far.

## HOMEWORK

In addition to completing the exercises on page 19 of their *early bird* books, ask the children to finish off their individual *favourites crests*. Encourage the children to ask their parents to sign their completed Workpage.

## ROUND UP

Teach the skipping rhyme *I like coffee, I like tea* using Unit 9, Part 4 on the Class Cassette. Get the children to skip with a real skipping rope. If you don't have a skipping rope, use mime instead.

*Tapescript*
*Unit 9, Part 4. Listen and join in.*

| | |
|---|---|
| I like coffee. I like tea. | I like Annie in with me. |
| I like coffee. I like tea. | I like Andy in with me. |
| I like coffee. I like tea. | I like Charlie in with me. |

## EVALUATION

In terms of evaluation of this Unit, the following table can be used as a guide. You may photocopy and include it in your school record book. For simplicity, tick a column if you are satisfied with a child's performance; leave it blank if you are not happy. *Note:* The table is a guide, and a record to refer back to. It is not intended as a grade list.

| Name | Activity completed | Can give the PR instructions for this Unit | Can understand your questions about favourites, likes and dislikes | Can give true responses | Can communicate information about favourites, likes and dislikes |
|---|---|---|---|---|---|
| | | | | | |
| | | | | | |
| | | | | | |
| | | | | | |
| | | | | | |
| | | | | | |
| | | | | | |
| | | | | | |
| | | | | | |
| | | | | | |
| | | | | | |

# Unit 10   Making a Mask

## INTRODUCTION

This Unit introduces *shapes*, *sizes* and *materials*. The Unit deals with the theme of *faces* and focuses on:

- observing and drawing face shapes;
- sorting shapes and materials;
- making masks from card and *junk* materials;
- parts of the head and face.

Through the practical activities in Unit 10, the children will:

- describe shapes;
- describe sizes;
- describe materials;
- use *is/are* in the description of features;
- use *have/has* in the description of features;
- use *adjectives* to describe features;
- compare shapes and sizes;
- ask questions about shapes and sizes;
- consolidate their active recognition of a wide range of question forms in English.

Table 1 (below) summarises the content of the Unit. Table 2 gives an outline of the key teaching steps.

**Table 1**

| The Children's Experience of Language Input across the Curriculum | | | Language Output from the Children in an Activity-Based Context | |
|---|---|---|---|---|
| Activities and topics | Teacher's questions, instructions, and comments about: | Physical Response Activities | Vocabulary | Expressions and structures |
| face shapes; making a mask | observing face shapes; sorting shapes; making a mask | draw | *shape* round square triangle rectangle egg heart big medium sized small mask parts of the face ugly/pretty | I don't have . . . Can I borrow . . . ? Do/does questions he/she/it has a . . . I/you have a . . . |

**Table 2**

| Lesson 1<br>Preparation Activities | Lesson 2<br>Main Activity:<br>Making a Mask | Lesson 3<br>Follow Up Activities |
|---|---|---|
| Warm Up: drawing shapes on a friend's back | Warm Up: making *body shapes* | Warm Up: play *feeling faces* |
| Check Homework: review *favourites crests*; colour in *star 9* | Check Homework: display and identify the *junk* materials brought in | Check Homework: feedback on masks |
| Presenting New Language: shapes and parts of the face | Activity: the children make masks | Language Practice: describing masks and classmates |
| Game: play *Bingo* with shapes | Language Practice: *Does he, she or it . . . ?* | Unit 10 Workpage (Student's Book page 21): use Home Cassette Unit 10, Parts A and B |
| Review: Action Game: use Class Cassette Unit 7, Part 2 (follow Procedure 1) | Homework: finish off masks | Options: drawing own reflections in the mirror; silhouette drawings |
| Homework: bring in *junk* materials for the mask | Round Up: the children act out the rhyme *Grandma, what big eyes you've got* – use Class Cassette Unit 7, Part 5 | Homework: finish off Workpage (Student's Book page 21); bring in Picture Dicionaries |
| Round Up: drawing shapes on a friend's back | | Round Up: drawing shapes on a friend's back |

*Note:* The review Unit is Unit 7.

# Lesson 1
# Preparation Activities

## PREPARING YOUR LESSON

– Prepare flash cards and real items for the various shapes on page 20 of the Student's Book.

– Bring in an example selection of *junk* materials for demonstration purposes. The children will use these in Lesson 2 when they make their masks.

## WARM UP

*[handwritten: circle, square, rectangle, triangle oval, oblong, star heart, diamond]*

• previewing *shape* vocabulary
• friendship activity
• group formation activity

*[handwritten: draw shapes on board]*

Drawing shapes on a partner's back.

i. Demonstrate the activity with S1. You sit behind S1 and draw a shape on his or her back with your finger. Use the shapes that are on page 20 of the *early bird* book. S1 must guess the shape and draw it on the palm of your hand. You change roles and repeat the activity.

ii. Organise the children into pairs. S1 sits behind S2. Pairs do the finger drawing activity.

iii. The children change roles, then partners and repeat the activity.

## CHECK HOMEWORK

a) Encourage the children to describe their completed individual *favourites crests* on page 18 of their *early bird* books.

  i. You give the example. Point to your own *favourites crest* as you speak.
T: *This is my crest. My favourite food is chocolate cake. My favourite colour is yellow. My favourite drink is wine.*

  ii. You repeat your description, leaving out key words. The class says the missing words.
T: *This is my . . .*
Ss: *Favourites crest.*
T: *My favourite food . . .*
Ss: *Is chocolate cake . . . etc.*

  iii. S1 comes to the front of the class, holds up his or her crest and points to his or her favourite items. The class describes them. Repeat this activity with a new S1.

  iv. Organise the children into groups of three or four. The children take turns to describe their crests to their group. You go round and help with the language. Whenever feasible say a complete description while the children are listening. Then let them try. Encourage student-to-student correction rather than allowing the children merely to repeat line by line after you.

b) Grading Unit 9.

  i. Show your completed pages for Unit 9. As in previous Units, ask the children what colour (grade) you deserve for your work. Turn to the *star chart* on the inside back cover of the book. Abide by the class decision on your grade, and colour in *star 9* on the star chart.

  ii. Ask the children to work in pairs. The children colour in their partner's *star* for this Unit. If there is any dispute, ask another child to be the final judge of grade.

  iii. Check that parents have signed their children's Workpage.

## PRESENTING NEW LANGUAGE

Teach the shapes on page 20 of the *early bird* book. Also review parts of the face. Use flash cards, drawings and real items as teaching aids for the shapes. Use flash cards, drawings and real faces for the parts of the face.

i. Show your flash cards in random order to the children. Ask all the children to copy the flash card of their choice onto a blank piece of paper. When finished, the children put these into their pockets for later.

ii. Organise the class into a semi-circle. Give out the picture flash cards of the shapes and parts of the face (at random) to the children. (One child takes responsibility for one word.) You name the shape or part of the face as you give out the card. The children listen only.

iii. You name the shapes and parts of the face. The children hold up the appropriate flash card. They don't speak.

iv. You name the shapes. The children with the shape or part of the face flash cards hold them up. The remainder of the class draw the shape in the air with their fingers, or touch the correct part of their faces. They don't speak at this stage.

v. Ask the children to put their flash cards in various locations around the classroom. Organise the class into groups of two or three. Ask groups to stand near specific flash cards. You then name the shape or part of the face. Groups must form the outline of their shape or part of the face with their arms, hands, and bodies.

vi. Ask the children to move to another flash card of their choice and repeat the activity.

vii. Ask the children to stand in a circle. You choose one flash card. You walk around the group with this flash card and teach it to various children. You encourage all the children to do the same with the flash cards they drew at the beginning of this activity.
T–S1: *Mine is a rectangle*
S1–T: *(Mine is) a triangle.*
T–S2: *Mine is a rectangle.*
S2–T: *(Mine is) a square . . . etc.*
You move into the background as this activity gathers momentum. Encourage the children to help and correct each other.

viii. *Consolidation step:* You stop the activity. You name each of the shapes and parts of the face. The children must hold up their flash cards when they hear their word. The children then exchange flash cards and repeat the activity.

## GAME

- consolidating *shapes* vocabulary
- consolidating *big, medium sized* and *small*
- listening skills

Play *Shapes bingo*.

i. Draw, or ask the children to draw *big, medium sized*, and *small* shapes (from page 20) on the board.

ii. Ask the children to choose any three shapes and draw them on a sheet of their own paper. While the children are doing this, make your own drawings of all the shapes on small pieces of paper.

iii. Put your *shapes* into a bag or box. When the children are ready, you pick out shapes from the bag, and call them out. The children check their drawings as you call them. The first child to match his or her three drawings wins a prize (e.g. a sweet), and becomes the caller for a repeat game.

## REVIEW

Review the Action Game for Unit 7. Follow Procedure 1 on page 15. Use Unit 7, Part 2 on the Class Cassette.

*Tapescript*
*Unit 7, Part 2. Listen and do the actions.*
Ready? Stand up please. Come here. Pick up three numbers. Say the whole number. Now put the numbers down.

## HOMEWORK

i. Ask the children to find and bring in objects for each shape: *round, square, egg shaped, triangle shaped . . . etc.* for the next lesson. Show and pass round examples of the shapes you want.

ii. Ask the children to bring in *junk* materials for their mask work in the next lesson. Once again, show examples of what you want them to bring.

## ROUND UP

Repeat the Warm Up activity you did at the beginning of this lesson.

# Lesson 2
# Making a Mask

## PREPARING YOUR LESSON

– Prepare large sheets of thin card or thick paper for the children to make masks out of.

– Prepare glue, coloured paper, scraps of wool, card, string, elastic and other *junk* materials for the masks.

– Bring in plenty of old newspaper to cover the working areas.

– Prepare your own mask for demonstration purposes.

## WARM UP

The children make shapes with their bodies.

i.  Organise the children into pairs or groups of three. You give the instructions to make specific shapes. They make the shapes as a pair or group.
T: *Make a big round shape with your arms. Now make a tiny, tiny square shape . . . etc.*

ii.  Choose S1. S1 gives the instructions (with your help). Pairs and groups make the shapes.

## CHECK HOMEWORK

Sort and display the items and shapes that the children have brought in. Consolidate relevant language.

i.  You name and identify the items and shapes and materials. The children watch and listen.
T: *This is a very small round shaped object. It's made of plastic. This is a medium sized square shaped object . . . etc.*

ii.  You repeat your description, leaving out key words. The class says the missing words.
T: *This is a very small . . .*
Ss: *Round shaped object . . . etc.*

iii.  S1 comes to the front of the class. S1 holds up objects. The class describes them. Repeat this activity with a new S1.

iv.  Organise the children into groups of three or four. Give a selection of objects to the children. They take turns to describe the shapes of the objects to their group. You go round and help with the language. Whenever feasible say a complete description while the children are listening. Then let them try. Encourage student-to-student correction rather than allowing the children merely to repeat line by line after you.

v.  Get the children to sort the items into sets based on similar shaped or sized material. Mark off areas of the floor, or table top with string or cotton. Make these areas the same shape as the items the children will be sorting. The children place the items inside these areas according to shape or size.

vi.  When finished, ask the children questions about the sets.

## ACTIVITY

• making masks from various *junk* materials
• using shape, size and colour
• sorting and classifying shapes
• describing masks
• practising *classroom language*
• asking *shape* and *size* questions

The children make masks.    *children draw a big face with shapes. Demo.*

a) Preparing the children for the activity.

i.  Look carefully at the faces of the children in your class. Draw the most common *face shapes* on the board. For example, *round, egg shaped, triangle shaped*. Draw the shapes far enough apart so that the children will be able to stand in front of their face shape, then ask them to do so.

ii.  Check that all the children agree that everyone is standing in the correct *shape* group.

iii.  When everyone agrees, count the total numbers of children under each shape and record this information on a simple class chart on the board.

b) The children make masks.

i.  Demonstrate and explain what you want the children to do. Make all necessary materials (scissors, glue, large sheets of paper or card, *junk* materials) available on a central table or desk.

ii. Divide the class into groups of four or five. Appoint a group leader who also acts as a *tidy monitor*. Explain and demonstrate the aims of the activity: to make a mask that looks like a classmate. Explain that each child must make a mask. Groups discuss the materials they need (mother tongue). Group leaders collect the materials from the materials table.

iii. You go round and chat to the groups in English while they are working. Ask them questions, make comments, using lots of gestures to help explain your meaning.

iv. Display the masks when the children have finished.

## LANGUAGE PRACTICE

- practising *Does he/she/it have . . . ?* questions
- feedback on the masks
- consolidating *shapes* and *face* vocabulary

Assign each of the children's masks a *picture number*. Bear in mind that pictures 1–3 (on the Cassette) are male, and pictures 4–6 are female. Use Unit 10, Part 1 on the Class Cassette.

i. Play the Cassette. Point to a mask. The children answer the questions on the Cassette.

*Tapescript*
*Unit 10, Part 1. Listen, look at each picture. Say yes or no.*
Picture 1. Does he have a round shaped face?
Picture 2. Does he have a square shaped nose?
Picture 3. Does he have two triangle shaped eyes?
Picture 4. Does she have a heart shaped mouth?
Picture 5. Does she have a rectangle shaped face?
Picture 6. Does she have two square shaped ears?

Make up additional questions of your own.

ii. Organise the children into a semi-circle. Ask them to look at their masks. They listen to the questions. Choose children to answer the questions on the Cassette.

iii. Organise the children into groups of three or four. Choose a leader for each group. Play the Cassette again. Pause the Cassette after each question, rewind and play the question again, encouraging the leaders to ask the questions with the Cassette. Group members answer. Don't correct errors at this stage.

iv. Change leaders. Repeat the activity without the Cassette. You go round the class and help with the language if needed. As before, don't encourage the children merely to repeat after you.

## GAME

Play *Drawing in the mirror*. Use Unit 10, Part 2 on the Class Cassette.

i. The children stand in pairs. S1 of each pair follows the instructions on the Cassette. S2 of each pair is a *mirror*. S1 and S2 face each other and touch fingers. You play the Cassette. S1 draws the shape. S2 follows S1's movements like a mirror.

*Tapescript*
*Unit 10, Part 2. Listen and draw the right shape with your finger.*
1. Draw a big round shaped face.
2. Draw two small round shaped eyes.
3. Draw two small triangle shaped eyebrows.
4. Draw a big egg shaped nose.
5. Draw a small heart shaped mouth.
6. Draw two small square shaped ears.

ii. Repeat the activity. This time S2 stands in front of S1. S1 draws the face on S2's back with his or her finger.

iii. The children change partners. S1 gives S2 the drawing instructions without support from the Cassette. This is a free stage. Encourage the children to experiment. Don't correct errors.

iv. Finally, the class gives you the instructions. You draw the face on the board.

## HOMEWORK

Ask the children to finish off their masks at home.

## ROUND UP

Review and act out *Grandma, what big eyes you've got*. Refer back to Unit 7, Lesson 2 for the script.

# Lesson 3
# Follow Up Activities

## PREPARING YOUR LESSON

– Prepare your own Workpage, Student Book page 21 for demonstration purposes.

– Bring in a mirror and some lipstick. Bring in tracing paper.

– Bring in enough blindfolds for a quarter of the class.

## WARM UP

Play *Feeling faces.*

i. Blindfold S1. S1 feels the face of another child and guesses who it is.

ii. Divide the class into two teams. Team 1 stands in a group. Team 2 works in pairs.

iii. S1 from each pair in Team 2 blindfolds his or her partner (S2). S1 leads S2 to a member of Team 1 (S3).

iv. S2 feels S3's face for five seconds.

v. S1 takes S2 away from Team 1.

vi. The children remove their blindfolds and must find the face they felt.

vii. The children change roles and repeat this activity.

## CHECK HOMEWORK

Display masks and face shapes. Ask the children lots of questions about the masks. For example:
T: *Whose is this mask?*
S: *Anton's.*
T: *Anton, is this Anita's face?*
S: *No. It's Ken's.*
T: *What shape is Ken's mouth?*
S: *Heart shaped.*
T: *Do you agree, Maria? What shape is Ken's mouth?*
S: *Heart shaped . . . etc.*

## LANGUAGE PRACTICE

Ask the children to talk about the mask they have made.

i. You give the example. Point to your mask as you speak. For example:
T: *This is my mask. It's Maggie's face. She has a triangle shaped nose. She has two egg shaped eyes. She has a rectangle shaped mouth. Her hair is made of wool. She's beautiful.*

ii. You repeat your description, leaving out key words. The class says the missing words.
T: *This is my . . .*
Ss: *Mask.*
T: *It's . . .*
Ss: *Maggie's face . . . etc.*

iii. S1 comes to the front of the class. S1 points to his or her mask. The class describes it. Repeat this activity with a new S1.

iv. Organise the children into groups of three or four. The children take turns to describe their masks to their group. You go round and help with the language. Whenever feasible say a complete description while the children are listening. Then let them try. Encourage student-to-student correction rather than allowing the children merely to repeat line by line after you.

v. Choose and encourage the children to talk about their friends' faces to the rest of the class. Allow errors. Don't correct the children as they speak. If necessary, repeat your complete description of your own mask, while the children listen.

## WORKPAGE

Complete the Workpage, Student's Book page 21. Use Unit 10, Parts A and B on the Home Cassette. Explain and demonstrate what to do. Assign the exercises for homework.

*Tapescript*
*Unit 10, Part A. Listen and shade in yes or no.*
Picture 1. Does he have a round shaped face?
Picture 2. Does he have a square shaped nose?
Picture 3. Does he have two triangle shaped eyes?
Picture 4. Does she have a heart shaped mouth?
Picture 5. Does she have a rectangle shaped face?
Picture 6. Does she have two square shaped ears?

*Unit 10, Part B. Listen. Draw the face.*
1. Draw a big round shaped face.
2. Draw two small round shaped eyes.
3. Draw two small triangle shaped eyebrows.
4. Draw a big egg shaped nose.
5. Draw a small heart shaped mouth.
6. Draw two small square shaped ears.

Assign Part C (the face crossword) for homework.

## OPTIONS

a) Ask the children to draw round the outline of their reflections in the mirror.

i. Use the mirror and lipstick you have brought in. The children take turns to draw round the reflection of their faces.

ii. Put tracing paper over the lipstick outline. Copy the outline onto the tracing paper. Display the results.
*Note:* This activity can also be assigned for homework.

b) If you have a suitable light source, for example, an overhead projector light, the children can produce silhouettes.
Put paper on the wall. Draw round the silhouettes. Display the drawings.

## HOMEWORK

In addition to completing the exercises on page 21 of their *early bird* books, ask the children to bring in their Picture Dictionaries for the next lesson. Encourage the children to ask their parents to sign their completed Workpage.

## ROUND UP

a) Drawing shapes on a partner's back. Use Unit 10, Part 2 on the Class Cassette.

*Tapescript*
*Unit 10, Part 2. Listen and draw the right shape with your finger.*
1. Draw a big round shaped face.
2. Draw two small round shaped eyes.
3. Draw two small triangle shaped eyebrows.
4. Draw a big egg shaped nose.
5. Draw a small heart shaped mouth.
6. Draw two small square shaped ears.

i. Organise the class into two teams. The children stand in two team lines facing the board. The front child from each team has a piece of chalk and stands at the board.

ii. Starting at the back of the line, and ending at the board, the children draw on the backs of the children standing in front of them. The front child draws on the board.

b) Drawing the same face.
Organise the class into threes. S1 secretly draws a face and parts of the face on a sheet of paper, giving S2 and S3 the instructions necessary to draw an identical face. S2 and S3 draw on sheets of paper without showing each other their drawings. When finished, the three children compare their drawings. This is a free stage. Encourage the children to experiment. Don't correct errors.

## EVALUATION

In terms of evaluation of this Unit, the following table can be used as a guide. You may photocopy and include it in your school record book. For simplicity, tick a column if you are satisfied with a child's performance; leave it blank if you are not happy.
*Note:* The table is a guide, and a record to refer back to. It is not intended as a grade list.

| Name | Activity completed | Can give instructions to draw face shapes | Can understand your questions about face shapes | Can give true responses | Can describe a friend's face |
|------|--------------------|-----------------------------------------|-----------------------------------------------|------------------------|------------------------------|
|      |                    |                                         |                                               |                        |                              |
|      |                    |                                         |                                               |                        |                              |
|      |                    |                                         |                                               |                        |                              |
|      |                    |                                         |                                               |                        |                              |
|      |                    |                                         |                                               |                        |                              |
|      |                    |                                         |                                               |                        |                              |
|      |                    |                                         |                                               |                        |                              |

# Unit 11    Picture Dictionary Work

## INTRODUCTION

This is the third Dictionary Unit in the course. The aims are as follows:

- giving the children further practice of dictionary skill activities;

- encouraging the children to continue their own, independent Picture Dictionary;

- consolidating awareness of an alphabetical filing system;

- giving further practice of spelling in English;

- reviewing and previewing vocabulary.

Table 1 (below) summarises the content of the Unit. Table 2 gives an outline of the key teaching steps.

**Table 1**

| The Children's Experience of Language Input across the Curriculum | | | Language Output from the Children in an Activity-Based Context | |
|---|---|---|---|---|
| Activities and topics | Teacher's questions, instructions, and comments about: | Physical Response Activities | Vocabulary | Expressions and structures |
| Picture Dictionary | sorting and classifying words; using a dictionary | Review | Review of foods, drinks, colours and games | Do you want a . . . or a . . . ? (four) of us How many . . . ? some/any |
| | | | | Review of present simple and future (going to) |

**Table 2**

| Lesson 1<br>Preparation Activities | Lesson 2<br>Main Activity:<br>Picture Dictionary Work | Lesson 3<br>Follow Up Activities |
|---|---|---|
| Warm Up: play<br>*Imaginary volleyball* | Warm Up: play *Pass the orange* | Warm Up: play *Chinese whispers – do you like . . .?* |
| Check Homework: colour in *star 10*; review the children's Picture Dictionaries | Check Homework and Role Play: sort the containers and wrappers the children have brought in; shopping requests – use Class Cassette Unit 11, Part 1; role play | Check Homework: language practice using the children's own Picture Dictionaries; review – use Class Cassette Unit 11, Part 4 |
| Presenting New Language: colours, foods, games and toys; recognition of spellings | Activity: the children sort and file the items on Unit 11 Activity Page (Student's Book page 39); cut out items on page 41 | Language Practice: describing pages in the Picture Dictionary |
| Role Play: shopping – use Class Cassette Unit 11, Part 1 | Language Practice: use Class Cassette Unit 11, Part 2 | Unit 11 Workpage (Student's Book page 23): use Home Cassette, Unit 11, Parts A, B and C |
| Review: Unit 7 – elephants | Game: play *Bingo* with the vocabulary items from Unit 11 | Game or Song: free choice |
| Homework: bring in Picture Dictionaries; bring in empty containers and wrappers for a shopping role play | Homework: file the items from page 41 into own Picture Dictionaries | Homework: finish off Workpage (Student's Book page 23) |
| Round Up: the children skip to the rhyme *I like coffee, I like tea* – use Class Cassette Unit 9, Part 4 | Round Up: play *Scissors, stone, paper* | Round Up: the children sing *I'm a little teapot* – use Class Cassette Unit 11, Part 5 |

*Note:* The review Unit is Unit 7.

# Lesson 1
# Preparation Activities

## PREPARING YOUR LESSON

– Prepare picture flash cards or real items for the vocabulary items on page 39 of the Student's Book.

– Prepare *word* flash cards for the vocabulary.

– Bring in empty food and drink containers for the shopping role play.

– Bring in a skipping rope.

– Read through the Introduction and teaching notes for Unit 4.

## WARM UP

Play an *imaginary* game of volleyball.

i. Organise the class into two teams. Decide where the net is. Make sure the players consider the position of the ball, and other players during this activity.

ii. Repeat the activity with a game of doubles tennis.

## CHECK HOMEWORK

a) Grading Unit 10.

i. Show your completed pages for Unit 10. As in previous Units, ask the children what colour (grade) you deserve for your work. Turn to the *star chart* on the inside back cover of the book. Abide by the class decision on your grade, and colour in *star 10* on the star chart.

ii. Ask the children to work in pairs. The children colour in their partner's *star* for this Unit. If there is any dispute, ask another child to be the final judge of grade.

iii. Check that parents have signed their children's Workpage.

b) Checking the children's Picture Dictionaries.

i. Organise the children into pairs or threes. Ask them to look at each other's Picture Dictionaries. This is a free stage. Allow the children about five minutes to exchange ideas and information.

ii. Make sure that the children who have forgotten their Picture Dictionaries, bring them in for the next lesson.

## PRESENTING NEW LANGUAGE

a) Teach the new items on page 39 of the Student's Book. Use your picture flash cards and real items for the vocabulary items as teaching aids.

i. Show and name the items or flash cards. The children watch and listen only.

ii. Ask the children to pick up and give items to other children.
T: *Rikki. Pick up the cookie. Give it to Yoshiko . . . etc.*

iii. Ask the children to identify the items they are holding. Use gestures to help explain your meaning.
T: *Who has the crisps? Me or you?*
S: *Me.*
T: *Eva. Who has the coffee?*
S: *Toni . . . etc.*

iv. Ask the children to stand in a circle. You choose one flash card or item. You walk around the group with this flash card and teach it to various children. You encourage all the children to do the same with the flash cards or items they are holding. Move into the background as this activity gathers momentum. Encourage the children to help and correct each other.

v. *Consolidation step:* You stop the activity. You name each of the items. The children hold their item or flash card above their heads when they hear their word. The children then exchange flash cards and items, and repeat the activity.

b) Focus on spelling[1].
Organise the class into two teams. The teams stand or sit in a large semi-circle. Collect in all the picture flash cards (and items) and lay them face down on the floor or desks. Display the *word* flash cards, word upwards, on the floor or desks. The children from each team take turns to compete against each other in a variety of mini-challenges. For example:

i. You name a vocabulary item. The first child to touch the word for that item scores a team point – if he or she can match the spelling to the real item or picture of the item.

ii. You start to spell a word. The first child to guess the word you are spelling scores a team point.

---

[1] Spelling may be inappropriate for younger children, in which case omit this activity for the time being.

iii. You ask the two competing children to close their eyes. Ask them how to spell one word each. Correct spelling scores a point.
T: *How do you spell crayon? . . . etc.*

iv. Ask S1 to take your role. He or she asks the spelling questions. Don't correct while S1 is speaking. If there are errors, when a child has finished, and before asking a new student to be the teacher, you have another turn. In this way you give the class another chance to listen to a correct example.

v. Finally, organise the children into pairs. The children turn to page 39. S1 asks a spelling. S2 spells the word without looking at the page. For example:
S1: *How do you spell coffee?*
S2: *c. . .o. . .f. . .f. . .e. . .e . . . etc.*

## ROLE PLAY

- dramatising a dialogue
- reviewing vocabulary
- introducing *some/any*

Encourage the children to do a *shopping* role play. Use Unit 11, Part 1 on the Class Cassette.

i. Set up a corner-shop scene. Adapt the class layout to represent shelves, counters, and the cash desk. The class door is the entrance to the shop.

ii. Confirm that all the children know the shop layout.

iii. Choose three children to demonstrate the role play. Assign the *shopping* roles of sales assistant (S3), cashier (S2) and shopper (S1).

iv. You play the Cassette. The three children do the actions and mime the situation. They don't speak at this stage.

*Tapescript*
*Unit 11, Part 1. Listen and ask your friend for the right pictures.*
1. Can I have some chocolate and some ice-cream and some coke please?
2. Can I have some cookies and some crisps and some milk please?

v. Play the Cassette again. Pause the Cassette after each request, rewind and play the request again, encouraging S1 to ask for items with the Cassette. Encourage S3 to greet S1 (*Good morning. Can I help you?*) and to use *Here you are* when handing items to S1. Similarly, encourage S2 to thank (*Thank you*) S1 on receipt of money.

vi. Ask a new group of children to do the role play. The rest of the class observes.

vii. Organise the class into groups of three. The groups rehearse the role play. You go round the class and help with the language if needed. As before, don't encourage the children merely to repeat after you. Give the children complete examples to listen to, leave the group, and allow them time to practise.

viii. Encourage groups to do the role play in front of the class. Don't correct errors while the children are speaking.

## REVIEW

- reviewing the use of the present simple (*an elephant lives in . . . ; an elephant eats . . .*)
- reviewing numbers and dimensions

Review Unit 7. Encourage the children to ask each other questions about real elephants.

i. Organise the children into a semi-circle. Ask them to turn back to Unit 7, pages 14 and 15. Ask them questions. Elicit the information (food, measurements, etc.) they found out about elephants in Unit 7. Write up this information on the board.

ii. Organise the children into groups of three or four. Choose a leader for each group. Ask questions about elephants. Repeat the questions, encouraging the leaders to ask the questions with you. Group members answer. Don't correct errors at this stage.

iii. Change leaders. Repeat the activity.

iv. Change leaders. Leaders ask questions without your support.

## HOMEWORK

i. Ask the children to bring in empty cans, packets and wrappers for the role play in the next lesson.

ii. Remind the children to bring their Picture Dictionaries for the next lesson.

## ROUND UP

- reviewing the present simple (I like . . . )

Review the skipping rhyme from Unit 9, Part 4 on the Class Cassette: *I like coffee, I like tea.* Get the children to skip with a real skipping rope. If you don't have a skipping rope, use mime instead.

*Tapescript*
*Unit 9, Part 4. Listen and join in.*

| | |
|---|---|
| I like coffee. I like tea. | I like Annie in with me. |
| I like coffee. I like tea. | I like Andy in with me. |
| I like coffee. I like tea. | I like Charlie in with me. |

# Lesson 2
# Picture Dictionary Work

## PREPARING YOUR LESSON

- Prepare a large flash card for the new heading on page 22: *games and toys*. One method is to make an enlarged photocopy of the heading, and glue it onto thin card.

- Bring in the flash cards and real items that you used last lesson.

- Bring in your flash cards (from Unit 4) for the headings *colours* and *food and drink*.

## WARM UP

Play *Pass the orange (or ball)*.

i. Organise the class into two teams. The teams stand in two lines.

ii. The children in each team pass the orange or ball from child to child without using their hands or arms. For example, they pass it under their chins or between their knees.

## CHECK HOMEWORK AND ROLE PLAY

i. Sort and display the items brought in.

ii. Decide whether you need to teach the English name for any of the new items brought in for the role play. (Since the whole class will not need all the items, it may be more practical to teach specific vocabulary to the small groups while they are rehearsing.)

iii. Review the role play based on Unit 11, Part 1 on the Class Cassette.

*Tapescript*
*Unit 11, Part 1. Listen and ask your friend for the right pictures.*
1. Can I have some chocolate and some ice-cream and some coke please?
2. Can I have some cookies and some crisps and some milk please?

iv. Set up a corner-shop scene as in last lesson.

v. Confirm that all the children know the shop layout.

vi. Choose three children to demonstrate the role play. Assign the *shopping* roles of sales assistant (S1), cashier (S2) and shopper (S3).

vii. You play the Cassette. The class listens, then the three children act out the situation.

viii. Organise the class into groups of three. The groups rehearse the role play. You go round the class and help with the language if needed. As before, don't encourage the children merely to repeat after you. Give the children complete examples to listen to, leave the group, and allow them time to practise.

ix. Encourage groups to do the role play in front of the class. Don't correct errors while the children are speaking.

## ACTIVITY

Dictionary work with the items on page 39 of the Student's Book.

a) Teach the new Picture Dictionary heading *games and toys* on page 22. Review the *colours* and *food and drink* headings.

   i. Organise the class into a large semi-circle.

   ii. You show and name each *heading* flash card. The children watch and listen only.

   iii. Display the headings on the board or the wall. Ask the children to point to the various headings. The children don't speak at this stage.

   iv. Ask the children to stand under headings.
T: *Jeanne, stand under the games and toys heading. Marianne, stand under the colours heading . . . etc.*

   v. Ask the children to identify the headings:
T: *Who's standing under the colours heading? Hands up. What heading is Maria standing under, Pepi?*
S: *Games and toys . . . etc.*

b) Cutting out the items.

   i. Organise the class into groups of four. The children sit in their groups. Choose a *tidy monitor* for each group.

   ii. Check that all groups have access to a pair of scissors.

   iii. Ask the children to turn to pages 39 and 41 of their *early bird* books. Point out the differences between pages 39 and 41.

iv. Give instructions to cut out items from page 39.
T: *Does everybody have a pair of scissors? Everyone hold up your scissors. Now, cut out the cookie. Only the cookie... What picture are we going to cut out next? The sandwich or water or lemonade or...?*
S: *Sandwich.*
T: *Hands up if you think we're going to cut out the sandwich next... Well you're right. We're going to cut out the sandwich. Everybody cut out the sandwich... etc.*

v. Give these types of instructions for four items, then ask the children to continue cutting out the rest of the items by themselves. Go round the class while the children are working. Ask *going to* questions:
T: *What picture are you going to cut out next? Are you going to cut out the colour grey or white?*
Encourage the children to ask each other similar questions while they are working.

vi. Ask the children to cut up page 41. They put these items in their *bits and pieces* envelopes. When they have finished, organise the class into a semi-circle.

c) Sorting and filing the items from page 39 onto page 22 of the *early bird* Student's Book.

i. Put your flash cards of the headings on the board.

ii. Show the flash cards for the vocabulary items. Ask the children to put the flash cards of the vocabulary items under the correct heading.
T: *What's this, Miki?*
S: *A cookie.*
T: *Where does the cookie go? Which heading? Food and drink, games and toys, or...? Where does it go? Show me.*
S: *Here... etc.*

*Note:* Encourage the children to suggest more than one *filing* alternative. For example, *running* and *swimming* could reasonably be filed under a new heading of *sports*. If the children wish to do this, make extra photocopies of the items and encourage the children to design their own separate new headings.

iii. The class work in their groups and sort all their items from page 39 under the headings printed on page 22. You go round and ask questions about the vocabulary and the classification of the items.
T: *What's this called in English?*
S: *Crisps.*
T: *Which heading does it go under?*
S: *Food and drink... etc.*

## LANGUAGE PRACTICE

- offering and accepting food or drink
- reviewing the question form of the present simple: *Do you want...?*
- consolidating use of *or...*

i. Organise the class into pairs. The children take out their dictionary items from their *bits and pieces* envelopes.

ii. Play Unit 11, Part 2 on the Class Cassette. Stop the Cassette after each question. The children choose what they want and hold up the appropriate picture.

*Tapescript*
*Unit 11, Part 2. Listen and say what you want.*
1. Do you want some lemonade or orange juice?
2. Do you want a sandwich or a cookie?
3. Do you want a coke or a glass of water?

iii. Choose S1. Replay the Cassette. S1 asks the questions with the Cassette. You give S1 the appropriate pictures, and a short response.
S1: *Do you want some lemonade or orange juice?*
T: *Some lemonade, please.*

iv. Change S1. Repeat the activity. This time S1 chooses children to answer the questions.

v. Pairwork. Repeat the activity without the Cassette.

vi. The children return their items to the *bits and pieces* envelope at the end of the activity.

## GAME

- reviewing vocabulary
- focusing on listening skills

Play *Bingo* with the vocabulary items on page 41.

i. Ask the children to take out any three items from their *bits and pieces* envelopes and lay them face up in front of them.

ii. You put all your own pictures from page 41 into a bag or box. When the children are ready, you pick out the pictures one at a time from the bag, and call them out. The first child to match his or her three items wins a prize (e.g. a sweet), and becomes the caller for a repeat game.

## HOMEWORK

i.  Ask the children to glue the items from page 41 (which are now in their *bits and pieces* envelopes) into their Picture Dictionaries under the appropriate headings.

ii. Ask the children to draw (or find a cut-out from a magazine,) one additional item for their *colours, food and drink, games and toys* pages.

## ROUND UP

Play *Scissors, stone, paper*. The class plays the game in pairs:
S1 + S2: *Scissors, stone, paper!*
Refer back to the Round Up stage of Unit 4, Lesson 2 for the procedure.

# Lesson 3
# Follow Up Activities

## PREPARING YOUR LESSON

– Prepare your Workpage, Student's Book page 23 for demonstration purposes.

## WARM UP AND LANGUAGE PRACTICE

• reviewing the question form of the present simple
• reviewing the short answer form

a) Play *Chinese whispers* with *Do you like . . . ?* questions. For example:
T: *Do you like milk?*
For the procedure, refer back to Unit 1, Lesson 1.

b) Use Unit 11, Part 3 on the Class Cassette.

   i. Organise the class into a semi-circle. You play the Cassette. The children answer yes or no.

   *Tapescript*
   *Unit 11, Part 3. Listen and say yes or no.*
   1. Do you like milk?
   2. Do you like chocolate?
   3. Do you like swimming?
   4. Do you like skipping?

   ii. Divide the semi-circle into two teams. You play the Cassette. S1 from Team 1 asks the question with the Cassette. S2 from Team 2 must repeat the key word, and reply. Correct questions and answers score team points.
   S1: *Do you like chocolate?*
   S2: *Chocolate? Yes, I do.*

   iii. Organise the class into pairs. Repeat the activity without the Cassette. Go round the class and help where necessary.

## CHECK HOMEWORK

• reviewing the difference between *-ty* and *-teen* numbers
• practising dictionary skills

Check the children have filed the items correctly in their new Dictionaries. Use Unit 11, Part 4 on the Class Cassette.

i. Play the first example on the Cassette: *Water is number 16. 16.*
   Ask the children to find the correct page in their Picture Dictionary for *water*. They find the item *water*, and number it.

ii. Continue with the remaining examples in Part 4. The children find the appropriate Picture Dictionary page each time, and number the items according to the instructions on the Cassette.

*Tapescript*
*Unit 11, Part 4. Listen and write in the correct numbers on the pictures.*
Water is number 16. 16.
Computer games is number 60. 60.
Yellow is number 40. 40.
Grey is number 14. 14.
Purple is number 18. 18.
Black is number 30. 30.
White is number 90. 90.
Orange is number 19. 19.

## LANGUAGE PRACTICE

Ask the children to talk about the pages in their Picture Dictionary.

i.  You give the example. Point to your *food and drink* page as you speak.
    T: *This is my food and drink page. This is a picture of some cake. This is a picture of some ice-cream . . . etc.*

ii. You repeat your description, leaving out key words. The class says the missing words.
    T: *This is my . . .*
    Ss: *Food and drink page . . .*
    T: *This is a picture . . .*
    Ss: *Of some cake . . . etc.*

iii. S1 comes to the front of the class. S1 points to items on his or her *food and drink* page. The class describes them. Repeat this activity with a new S1 and a different Dictionary page.

iv. Organise the children into groups of three or four. The children take turns to describe the content of pages in their new Picture Dictionaries to their group. (Also encourage them to check each other's spellings.) You go round and help with the language. Whenever feasible say a complete description while the children are listening. Then let them try. Encourage student-to-student correction rather than allowing the children merely to repeat line by line after you.

v.  Choose and encourage the children to talk about Picture Dictionary pages to the rest of the class. Allow errors.

## WORKPAGE

- recording work done in this Unit
- reviewing and consolidating

Complete the Workpage, Student's Book page 23. Use Parts A, B and C on the Home Cassette.

a) Demonstrate how to do Part A. Do the first example of the exercise in class with the children. Assign the rest for homework.

   *Tapescript*
   *Unit 11, Part A. Listen. Draw the pictures. Write in the missing words. Then colour in your pictures.*
   1. Can I have some chocolate and some ice-cream and some coke, please?
   2. Can I have some cookies and some crisps and some milk, please?

b) Demonstrate how to do Part B. Use Unit 11, Part B on the Home Cassette. Show your own page 23 for demonstration purposes.

   i.  When the children understand what to do, organise the class into pairs.

   ii. You play the Cassette. Pause the Cassette after each instruction, rewind and play the instruction again, encouraging S1 of each pair to speak with the Cassette but not colour in at this stage. S2 says what he or she wants.

   *Tapescript*
   *Unit 11, Part B. Listen. Think what you want. Colour it in.*
   1. Do you want some lemonade or orange juice?
   2. Do you want a sandwich or a cookie?
   3. Do you want a coke or a glass of water?

   iii. The children change roles and repeat the activity. You go round the class helping where necessary. Finally, the children colour in their choices in each example.

c) Demonstrate how to do Part C. Use Unit 11, Part C on the Home Cassette. Show your own page 23 for demonstration purposes.

   *Tapescript*
   *Unit 11, Part C. Listen. Write yes or no.*
   1. Do you like milk?
   2. Do you like chocolate?
   3. Do you like swimming?
   4. Do you like skipping?

d) Demonstrate how to do Part D. The children must complete the missing information, and colour in where appropriate. Do the first example in class, and assign the remainder for homework.

## GAME OR SONG

Free choice. Ask the children if they want to play a game or repeat a rhyme. Suggest *Grandma, what big eyes you've got* (Unit 7, Lesson 2) or one of the games learnt previously.

## HOMEWORK

Ask the children to complete page 23 of their *early bird* books. Encourage the children to ask their parents to sign their completed Workpages.

## ROUND UP

Teach *I'm a little teapot* using Unit 1, Part 5 on the Class Cassette. Encourage the children to use lots of gestures while they sing.

*Tapescript*
*Unit 11, Part 5. Listen and join in.*
I'm a little teapot, short and stout.
Here's my handle. Here's my spout.
This is my saucer. This is my cup.
Pour in the milk and drink it up.

## EVALUATION

In terms of evaluation of this Unit, the following table can be used as a guide. You may photocopy and include it in your school record book. For simplicity, tick a column if you are satisfied with a child's performance; leave it blank if you are not happy. *Note:* The table is a guide, and a record to refer back to. It is not intended as a grade list.

| Name | Has sorted and classified items successfully | Is building up own Picture Dictionary | Can understand your questions about dictionary items | Can give true responses | Can communicate information about own Dictionary Pages |
|---|---|---|---|---|---|
| | | | | | |
| | | | | | |
| | | | | | |
| | | | | | |
| | | | | | |
| | | | | | |
| | | | | | |
| | | | | | |

# Unit 12   Working with Circle Shapes

## INTRODUCTION

This Unit reviews *shapes* and *sizes*. In particular the children are encouraged to examine the theme of *circles and ring (round) shapes*.

*Note*: The children cut up the *ring a ring of roses picture puzzle* on page 43 of the *early bird* Student's Book into individual pictures. Once cut out, and as a final activity, the *rhyme pictures* are assembled, in the correct order, onto the frame outlines printed on page 24.

The Activity Page, page 43, centres around the rhyme: *ring a ring of roses*. This rhyme refers to the Great Plague in England in the 17th century. A ring of roses was hung on the door of a house to show that the inhabitants were infected, 'Atishoo' shows sneezing as one of the signs of infection and 'We all fall down' refers to death caused by the infection. Although the rhyme is intended as an introduction and reference point to the main theme of *rings and circles*, the historical origin of the rhyme may be of interest to older children, especially if their country has suffered from a similar plague.

The children are involved in:

– observing and drawing round shapes;

– sorting shapes;

– making and measuring round shapes;

– singing *ring a ring of roses*.

Through the practical activities in Unit 12, the children will:

– describe shapes;

– measure and describe sizes;

– review *is/are* in the description of features;

– review *has/have* in the description of features;

– review *adjectives* to describe features;

– compare shapes and sizes;

– ask questions about shapes and dimensions;

– consolidate their active recognition of a wide range of question forms in English.

Table 1 (below) summarises the content of the Unit. Table 2 gives an outline of the key teaching steps.

### Table 1

| The Children's Experience of Language Input across the Curriculum | | | Language Output from the Children in an Activity-Based Context | |
|---|---|---|---|---|
| Activities and topics | Teacher's questions, instructions, and comments about: | Physical Response Activities | Vocabulary | Expressions and structures |
| *ring a ring of roses*; circle shapes | observing, sorting and classifying circle shapes; organising picture information | this way round the other way round throw watch catch | circle ring roses pocket long thin twisty balloon | both hands one hand ... plus ... equals wide/long<br><br>holding, walking, running ... etc. (present continuous) |

109

**Table 2**

| Lesson 1<br>**Preparation Activities** | Lesson 2<br>**Main Activity:**<br>**Working with Circle Shapes** | Lesson 3<br>**Follow Up Activities** |
|---|---|---|
| Warm Up: the children make *balloon shapes* with their bodies | Warm Up: play *Pass the balloon* | Warm Up: Action Game: use Class Cassette Unit 12, Part 1 (follow Procedure 3) |
| Check Homework: Picture Dictionary; colour in *star 11* | Check Homework: display and sort the circle shapes brought in | Check Homework: review *ring a ring of roses* |
| Presenting New Language: shapes and *ring a ring of roses* vocabulary | Activity 1: measuring circle shapes | Unit 12 Workpage (Student's Book page 25): use Home Cassette Unit 12, Parts A and D |
| Action Game: use Class Cassette Unit 12, Part 1 (follow Procedure 1) | Activity 2: play *ring a ring of roses* – use Class Cassette Unit 12, Part 2, cutting up Unit 12 Activity Page (Student's Book page 43) and reassembling the pieces | Language Practice and review: describing classmates |
| Review: Unit 9 – likes and dislikes | | Game: playing with hoops |
| Homework: bring in round shaped items | Homework: finish off assembling the pieces of the rhyme onto page 24 | Homework: finish off Workpage (Student's Book page 25) |
| Round Up: the children sing *I'm a little teapot* – use Class Cassette Unit 11, Part 5 | Round Up: drawing balloons on a friend's back | Round Up: the children make *balloon shapes* with their bodies |

*Note:* The review Unit is Unit 9.

# Lesson 1
# Preparation Activities

## PREPARING YOUR LESSON

– Bring in balloons of various sizes and colours.

– Bring in coins of various sizes and values.

– Bring in lots of round shaped objects.

– Prepare picture flash cards or items for each piece of the *ring a ring of roses* rhyme on page 43 of the Student's Book. One method is to make enlarged photocopies of the pieces and then ask the children to colour them in. Alternatively, ask the children to draw large copies for you in advance.

## WARM UP

The children make *balloon shapes* with their bodies.

i. You blow up balloons of various shapes and sizes. Focus the children's attention on the shapes.

ii. Blow up another balloon. The children *grow* as you blow up the balloon. For example:
*The children start curled up very small; they grow 'large and light' with rounded legs, puffed out cheeks and stomachs. The action stops when you stop blowing up the balloon.*

iii. The children imitate the movement of a balloon in the air. Focus on the *lightness* of a balloon in the air. For example:
*You throw the balloon high into the air. The children jump and turn. They land and stay still when you catch the balloon.*

iv. Let the air slowly out of the balloon. The children crumple slowly to the floor.

v. Let the air out quickly, and let the balloon fly around. The children whizz about.

vi. Pop the balloon. The children explode and crumple.

## CHECK HOMEWORK

i. Show your completed pages for Unit 11, and your Picture Dictionary. As for previous Units, ask the children what colour (grade) you deserve for your work. Turn to the *star chart* on the inside back cover of the *early bird* Student's Book. Abide by the class decision on your grade and colour in *star 11* on the star chart.

ii. Ask the children to work in pairs. The children colour in their partner's *star* for this Unit. If there is any dispute, ask another child to be the final judge of grade.

iii. Check that parents have signed their children's Workpage.

## PRESENTING NEW LANGUAGE

Teach the language for the rhyme: *ring, roses, pocket, posies.* Use flash cards and real objects as teaching aids.

i. Organise the class into a semi-circle. Show your flash cards in random order to the children. Ask all the children to copy the picture of their choice onto a blank piece of paper. When finished, the children put these into their pockets for later.

ii. Give out the picture flash cards and items at random to the children. (One child takes responsibility for one word.) You name the items as you give them out. The children listen only.

iii. You name the items. The children hold up the appropriate flash card or item. They don't speak.

iv. You name the items. The children with the flash cards or items hold them up. The rest of the class *mimes* the item. They don't speak at this stage.

v. Ask the children to put their flash cards or items in various locations around the classroom. Organise the class into groups of two or three. Ask groups to stand near specific flash cards or items. You name the items. Groups must form the shape of their item with their arms, hands, and bodies.

vi. Ask the children to move to another flash card or item of their choice and repeat the activity.

vii. Ask the children to stand in a circle. You choose one flash card. You walk around the group with this flash card and teach it to various children. You encourage all the children to do the same with the flash cards they drew at the beginning of this activity.
T–S1: *I have the roses.*
S1–T: *(I have) a pocket.*
T–S2: *I have the roses.*
S2–T: *(I have) the posies . . . etc.*
You move into the background as this activity gathers momentum. Encourage the children to help and correct each other.

viii. *Consolidation step:* You stop the activity. You name each item. The children must hold up their flash cards when they hear their word. The children then exchange flash cards and repeat the activity.

## ACTION GAME

Use Unit 12, Part 1 on the Class Cassette. Follow Action Game Procedure 1 on page 15.

*Tapescript*
*Unit 12, Part 1. You're going to play with a balloon. Listen and do the actions.*
*You're holding a big round red balloon. Hold it in both hands. Throw it high into the air. Watch it fall. Catch it. Put it down.*

## REVIEW

• reviewing *What's your favourite . . . ?*
• reviewing *likes* and *dislikes*

Review Unit 9. Encourage the children to ask each other questions about *favourites, likes* and *dislikes*.

i.  Organise the children into a semi-circle. Ask them to turn back to Unit 9, pages 18 and 19 in their *early bird* books. Ask them questions. Elicit the information about the class favourites as found out during Unit 9. Write up this information on the board.

ii. Organise the children into groups of three or four. Choose a leader for each group. Ask questions about favourites, likes and dislikes. Repeat the questions, encouraging the leaders to ask the questions with you. Group members answer. Don't correct errors at this stage.
T (+ leaders): *What's your favourite colour? Do you like yellow? What food don't you like? . . . etc.*

iii. Change leaders. Repeat the activity.

iv. Change leaders. Leaders ask questions without your support. You go round the class and help with the language if needed.

## HOMEWORK

Ask the children to bring *round shaped* objects for the next lesson. Show your own round shaped items as examples.

## ROUND UP

Review the song from Unit 11, Part 5 on the Class Cassette: *I'm a little teapot.*

# Lesson 2
# Working with Circle Shapes

## PREPARING YOUR LESSON

–  Bring in balloons of various shapes, sizes and colours.

–  Bring in lots of round shaped objects.

–  Bring in your picture flash cards or real items for the vocabulary of the rhyme *ring a ring of roses*.

–  Prepare *word* flash cards for each of the segments of the rhyme that correspond to the pieces.

## WARM UP

Play *Pass the balloon*.

i.  Organise the class into two teams. The teams stand in two lines.

ii. The children in each team pass a balloon from child to child without using hands or arms. For example, they pass it under their chins or between their knees.

## CHECK HOMEWORK

Sort and display the circle shapes and items that you and the children have brought in. For example, sort the objects into: *big circles and little circles; circles with holes and circles without holes.* Check that the children can recognise (but not necessarily name) the important objects.

i.  You name and identify the most common items. The children watch and listen.

ii. S1 comes to the front of the class and points to the items. You identify them.

iii. Repeat this activity with a new S1. This time the class identifies the items.

iv. Organise the children into groups of three or four. The children take turns to describe their items to their group. You go round and help with the language.

## ACTIVITY 1

a) The children measure the round objects.

  i. Organise the children into small groups. Appoint a leader for each group. Group leaders collect four round objects for their groups. Give each group a blank sheet of paper to record their results on.

  ii. The children measure round the edges of their objects and record their results on the group's sheet of paper. (Ask for ideas on how to do this. For example, using string or rolling the object along a tape measure.)

  iii. The children also measure how wide the objects are, once again recording the results.

  iv. Ask the children to divide the circumference by the width for each object. What do they find out? *(Note:* Circumference divided by width should always equal about 3.)

b) Language practice: Questions and answers on the results. For example:
  T: *How long is your cup round the edge?*
  S: *21 cm.*
  T: *Who has the biggest circle?*
  S: *Me.*
  T: *How wide is it across the middle? . . . etc.*

  i. Organise the children into new groups of four. Appoint new group leaders.

  ii. You ask the questions about the measurements. Use gestures to help you explain your questions. They answer.

  iii. Repeat your questions. Leaders ask the questions with you.

  iv. Groups change leaders. The new leaders ask similar questions without your support. You go round the class giving help where necessary. Encourage the children to use gestures and key words if they have problems with the language.

## ACTIVITY 2

The children learn *ring a ring of roses.* Use Unit 12, Part 2 on the Class Cassette.

  i. Organise the class into a semi-circle.

  ii. Use your picture flash cards of the rhyme. Play Unit 12, Part 2 on the Class Cassette. Hold up (point to) each piece of the rhyme as you play the Cassette. Also use gestures to help explain the meaning. The children watch and listen only at this stage.

  *Tapescript*
  *Unit 12, Part 2. Listen and hold up the right pieces.*
  Ring . . . a ring . . . of roses.
  A pocket full . . . of posies.
  A-tishoo . . . A-tishoo.
  We all . . . fall . . . down.

  iii. Play the Cassette again. Hold up two flash cards for each line of the rhyme, one of which is the correct picture. The children point to the correct one.

  iv. Mix your flash cards up. Lay them on the floor or your desk. Play the Cassette again. Ask the children to find and hold up the correct pictures.

  v. Organise the class into groups of three or four. Make sure all the children have access to a pair of scissors. Ask the children to turn to page 43 of their *early bird* books.

  vi. Ask them to cut up their rhymes. Ask the children who finish first to help slower classmates.

  vii. Organise the children into pairs. The children mix up their pictures and lay them face down. Play the Cassette again. The children take turns in finding and holding up the correct pictures to their partners.

  viii. Say the rhyme again. This time the children pick up the correct pieces and put them in their *bits and pieces* envelopes on the inside front cover of their books.

  ix. The children play *ring a ring of roses.* Use Unit 12, Part 3 on the Class Cassette.

  *Tapescript*
  *Unit 12, Part 3. Listen again. Learn the rhyme. Play the game.*
  Ring a ring of roses. A pocket full of posies. A-tishoo, A-tishoo. We all fall down.

  – You play the Cassette. The children link hands, listen, and go round in a circle in a clockwise direction, keeping time with the rhyme.

- Repeat the rhyme. The children listen again. Ask them to go the other way round.
- The children listen, go round in a circle and sing with the Cassette.

x. *Consolidation step*: The children play *Tiggy in the middle*.
- Lay out the flash card pieces of the rhyme in random order, in a big circle on the floor.
- S1 is *Tiggy* and stands in the middle of the circle. The other children stand behind the flash card pieces of the puzzle, one child per piece.
- One by one, the children say their piece of the rhyme in the correct order. *Tiggy* must run to the right piece each time.
- At the end of the rhyme change *Tiggy* and repeat the activity.

## HOMEWORK

Ask the children to glue the *ring a ring of roses* puzzle, and the rhyme itself, onto the outlines on page 24 of their books.

## ROUND UP

Drawing balloon shapes on a partner's back. Use Unit 12, Part 4 on the Class Cassette.

i. Organise the class into pairs. S1 of each pair stands behind S2. S1 *draws* the correct shaped balloon on S2's back. S2 touches the correct colours.

*Tapescript*
*Unit 12, Part 4. Listen. Draw the shape of the balloons with your finger.*
1. A big round red balloon.
2. A small heart shaped green balloon.
3. A long thin yellow balloon.
4. A long twisty purple balloon.

ii. Pairs change roles then partners and repeat the activity.

iii. Finally, before leaving the class, the children give you the drawing instructions. You draw the balloons on the board.

# Lesson 3
# Follow Up Activities

## PREPARING YOUR LESSON

- Prepare your Workpage, Student's Book page 25 for demonstration purposes.

- Bring in hoops, or make hoop shapes with string.

## WARM UP

Use Unit 12, Part 1 on the Class Cassette. Follow Action Game Procedure 3 on page 20.

*Tapescript*
*Unit 12, Part 1. You're going to play with a balloon. Listen and do the actions.*
You're holding a big round red balloon. Hold it in both hands. Throw it high into the air. Watch it fall. Catch it. Put it down.

## CHECK HOMEWORK

i. Make sure the children have glued in their picture puzzle for *ring a ring of roses*.

ii. Ask the children to sing and play *ring a ring of roses*.

## WORKPAGE

Complete the Workpage, Student's Book page 25. Use Unit 12, Parts A and D on the Home Cassette.

i. Explain and demonstrate what to do for Part A. Do the first two examples in class and assign the remainder for homework.

*Tapescript*
*Unit 12, Part A. Listen. Draw the balloons. Colour them in. Write in the missing words.*
1. A big round red balloon.
2. A small heart shaped green balloon.
3. A long thin yellow balloon.
4. A long twisty purple balloon.

ii. Assign Parts B and C for homework.

iii. Review (if necessary) the *Teach your parents* procedure for Part D. Refer back to Unit 2, Lesson 3. Assign the activity for homework.

*Tapescript*
*Unit 12, Part D. Listen. Teach your parents.*
You're holding a big round red balloon. Hold it in both hands. Throw it high into the air. Watch it fall. Catch it. Put it down.

## LANGUAGE PRACTICE AND REVIEW

Encourage the children to describe classmates.

i. You give the example. Describe one of the children. Use gestures to reinforce the meaning of your description. The children must guess who you are describing.
   T: *She's nine years old. She's about 143 centimetres tall. She has a round shaped face. She has brown eyes and brown hair. She's wearing a blue skirt. Who is she?*

ii. You repeat your description, leaving out key words. The class says the missing words.
   T: *She's nine . . .*
   Ss: *Years old.*
   T: *She's about . . .*
   Ss: *143 centimetres tall . . . etc.*

iii. S1 and S2 come to the front of the class. S1 points to various features of S2. The class describes them. Repeat this activity with a new S1.

iv. Organise the children into groups of three or four. The children take turns to describe one member of the class to their group. You go round and help with the language. Whenever feasible say a complete description while the children are listening. Then let them try. Encourage student-to-student correction rather than allowing the children merely to repeat line by line after you.

v. Choose and encourage the children to talk about a class friend to the rest of the class. Allow errors. Don't correct the children as they speak.

## GAME

Playing with hoops. Organise the class into two teams.

i. How many in a hoop?
   Find out which team can get the most children standing inside a hoop. Teams score one point for each member inside the hoop.

ii. Hoop jumps.
   Put the hoops in two long lines. The teams stand in two lines facing the hoops. S1 from Team 1, and S1 from Team 2 stand beside their first hoops. They must jump, feet together, from hoop to hoop, down the line of hoops without touching any edges, and then jump back to their original position. The second child from the team may then start jumping down the line of hoops. The winning team scores two points.

iii. Passing the hoop down the team.
   The children must pass the hoop down the team line by passing it over their bodies, and then stepping out of it. The winning team scores two points.

## HOMEWORK

Ask the children to complete page 25 of their *early bird* books. Encourage the children to ask their parents to sign their completed Workpage.

## ROUND UP

Repeat the Warm Up from Lesson 1 of this Unit: *balloon shapes.*

## EVALUATION

In terms of evaluation of this Unit, the following table can be used as a guide. You may photocopy and include it in your school record book. For simplicity, tick a column if you are satisfied with a child's performance; leave it blank if you are not happy.
*Note:* The table is a guide, and a record to refer back to. It is not intended as a grade list.

| Name | Measuring activities completed/ rhyme puzzle completed | Can give the PR instructions for this Unit | Can understand your questions about shapes and sizes | Can give true responses | Can describe a friend |
|---|---|---|---|---|---|
| | | | | | |
| | | | | | |
| | | | | | |

# Tapescripts

The following Tapescripts are for the Class Cassette. As the Home Cassette contains only extracts from the Class Cassette, they are not printed separately. Notes in brackets show which parts of the Class Cassette correspond to parts of the Home Cassette.

## Unit 1

(Class Cassette: Parts 3 and 4 = Home Cassette: Parts A and B)

*Unit 1, Part 1. Listen and do the actions.*
Put your hand up. Put your hand down.
Stand up. Come here. Go over there. Sit down.

*Unit 1, Part 2. Listen and do the actions.*
Reach up with your arms. Higher. Higher. Relax.
Now stretch your arms out. Wider. Wider. Relax.
Now. Right foot. Stand on your right foot, and hop.
1 . . . 2 . . . 3 . . . hop.
Left foot. Stand on your left foot. 1 . . . 2 . . . 3 . . . hop.
Now both feet. 1 . . . 2 . . . 3 . . . jump.
Now curl up. Really small. Smaller. Smaller. Relax.

*Unit 1, Part 3. Listen and give true answers.*
1. How old are you?
2. How tall are you?
3. How much do you weigh?
4. How long is your foot?

*Unit 1, Part 4. Listen and give true answers.*
1. How high can you reach?
2. How far can you stretch?
3. How high can you jump?
4. How far can you hop?

*Unit 1, Part 5. Listen and join in.*
One little, two little, three little indians . . .
Four little, five little, six little indians . . .
Seven little, eight little, nine little indians . . .
Ten little indian girls.

## Unit 2

(Class Cassette: Parts 2, 3 and 4 = Home Cassette: Parts A, B and C)

*Unit 2, Part 1. Listen and answer. Point to the right person each time.*
1. Who's the tallest in the class?
2. Who's the smallest?
3. Who has the longest foot?
4. Who can jump the highest?
5. Who can stretch the furthest?

*Unit 2, Part 2. Listen and do the actions.*
Stand over there, please. Back a bit. Good. Now smile. Say cheese. Thank you.

*Unit 2, Part 3. Look at your friend's photos and ask these questions.*
1. Who's this?
2. And who's this?

*Unit 2, Part 4. Look at your friend's photos and ask similar questions to these.*
1. Is this your sister?
2. Is this your friend?

*Unit 2, Part 5. Listen and join in.*
One, two, buckle my shoe. Three, four, knock at the door. Five, six, pick up sticks. Seven, eight, put them straight. Nine, ten, start again.

## Unit 3

(Class Cassette: Parts 2, 3 and 4 = Home Cassette: Parts A, B and C)

*Unit 3, Part 1. Listen and do the actions.*
Ready? Stand up please. Come here. Pick up a number. Say the number. Put the number down. Sit down.

*Unit 3, Part 2. Listen and draw the beetle.*
1. Draw one big head.
2. Draw two little eyes.
3. Draw two long antennae.
4. Draw one big, round body.
5. Draw six long legs.
6. Draw one little tail.

*Unit 3, Part 3. Throw a dice. Listen and say what number you throw each time.*
1. Throw the dice. What number did you get?
2. Throw the dice again. What number did you get this time?
3. Throw the dice again. What number did you get this time?

*Unit 3, Part 4. Throw a dice. Listen and answer yes or no.*
1. Throw the dice. Did you get a six?
2. Throw the dice again. Did you get a four?
3. Throw the dice again. Did you get a five?

*Unit 3, Part 5. Listen and join in.*
Head, body, legs and tail. Legs and tail.
Head, body, legs and tail. Legs and tail.
And eyes and ears and nose and nail.
Head, body, legs and tail. Legs and tail.

## Unit 4

(Class Cassette: Parts 1 and 3 = Home Cassette: Parts B and C)

*Unit 4, Part 1. Listen and count the right numbers.*
1. Count to 10.
2. Count to 20.
3. Count from 8 to 12.
4. Count from 6 to 15.

*Unit 4, Part 2. Listen, pick up the right picture. Hold it up.*
1. Hold up the hot dog, please.
2. Hold up the hamburger, please.
3. Hold up the ketchup, please.
4. Hold up the french fries, please.
5. Hold up something blue.
6. Hold up something pink.
7. Hold up something green.
8. Hold up something yellow.
9. Hold up something red.
10. Hold up the pizza.

*Unit 4, Part 3. Listen and do the actions.*
Ready? Put your hand up. Put your hand down.
Stand up. Come here. Go over there. Sit down. Thank you.

## Unit 5

(Class Cassette: Parts 1 and 2 = Home Cassette: Parts A and B)

*Unit 5, Part 1. Listen and spell these words.*
1. How do you spell yellow?
2. How do you spell blue?
3. How do you spell green?
4. How do you spell pink?

*Unit 5, Part 2. Listen, and say the right word.*
1. g...r...e...e...n      ...spells...
2. b...l...u...e          ...spells...
3. p...i...n...k          ...spells...
4. y...e...l...l...o...w  ...spells...

*Unit 5, Part 3. Listen and join in.*
One finger, one thumb, keep moving.
One finger, one thumb, keep moving.
One finger, one thumb, keep moving.
And off to town we go.
One finger, one thumb, one arm, keep moving.
One finger, one thumb, one arm, keep moving.
One finger, one thumb, one arm, keep moving.
And off to town we go.
One finger, one thumb, one arm, one leg, keep moving.
One finger, one thumb, one arm, one leg, keep moving.
One finger, one thumb, one arm, one leg, keep moving.
And off to town we go.
One finger, one thumb, one arm, one leg, one nod of the head, keep moving.
One finger, one thumb, one arm, one leg, one nod of the head, keep moving.
One finger, one thumb, one arm, one leg, one nod of the head, keep moving.
And off to town we go.
One finger, one thumb, one arm, one leg, one nod of the head, stand up, sit down, keep moving.
One finger, one thumb, one arm, one leg, one nod of the head, stand up, sit down, keep moving.
One finger, one thumb, one arm, one leg, one nod of the head, stand up, sit down, keep moving.
And off to town we go.
One finger, one thumb, one arm, one leg, one nod of the head, stand up, turn round, sit down, keep moving.
One finger, one thumb, one arm, one leg, one nod of the head, stand up, turn round, sit down, keep moving.
One finger, one thumb, one arm, one leg, one nod of the head, stand up, turn round, sit down, keep moving.
And off to town we go.

## Unit 6

(Class Cassette: Parts 1 and 3 = Home Cassette: Parts A (+B) and C)

*Unit 6, Part 1. Listen and do the actions.*
Ready? Pick up the hamburger. Pick up the ketchup. Squeeze the ketchup on the hamburger. Now open your mouth and bite.

*Unit 6, Part 2. Listen and hold up the right pictures.*
1.  This is Andy.
2.  This is Andy again.
3.  This is a hamburger.
4.  This is another hamburger.
5.  These are french fries.
6.  These are more french fries.
7.  Andy asks for a yummy hamburger.
8.  This is the ketchup.
9.  Andy puts lots of ketchup on the hamburger.
10. This is Annie.
11. This is Annie again.
12. Annie says 'Hi' to Andy. Andy jumps.
13. Oh no! The ketchup goes all over the man.

*Unit 6, Part 3. Listen to the story. Say the missing words.*
One day, Andy went to town. He went to a hamburger store. He was starving. He asked for a super big .........., super big .......... and lots and lots of .......... Yum. Andy picked up the hamburger and opened his mouth wide. Suddenly he felt a .......... on his shoulder. Andy jumped with surprise. He squeezed the hamburger hard. Oh no! The .......... went all over the man with the bald head.

## Unit 7

(Class Cassette: Parts 1 and 2 = Home Cassette: Parts A and B (+C))

*Unit 7, Part 1. Listen and write down the numbers you hear.*
Number 1. 17, 17
Number 2. 40, 40
Number 3. 30, 30
Number 4. 19, 19

*Unit 7, Part 2. Listen and do the actions.*
Ready? Stand up please. Come here. Pick up three numbers. Say the whole number. Now put the numbers down.

*Unit 7, Part 3. Listen and join the dots.*
Find the number 6. Ready? Listen to the numbers. Join up the dots. 6 . . . 2 . . . 0 . . . 17 . . . 9 . . . 16 . . . 20 . . . 1 . . . 13 . . . 10 . . . 4 . . . 7 . . . 12 . . . 3 . . . 18 . . . 5 . . . 19 . . . 28 . . . 11 . . . 14 . . . 15.
Now find the number 38. Ready? Listen to the numbers. Join the dots. 38 . . . 35 . . . 45 . . . 47 . . . 37 . . . 48 . . . 30 . . . 50 . . . 31 . . . 33 . . . 56 . . . 42 . . . 40 . . . 34 . . . 32 . . . 49 . . . 39 . . . 43 . . . 46 . . . 44 . . . 41.

*Unit 7, Part 4. Listen and colour your picture.*
1. Colour the left ear yellow.
2. Colour the right ear green.
3. Colour the trunk blue.
4. Colour the left legs pink.
5. Colour the right legs red.
6. Colour the tail brown.
7. Colour the head grey.

*Unit 7, Part 5. Listen and join in.*
Grandma, what big eyes you've got.
  –All the better to see you with.
Grandma, what big ears you've got.
  –All the better to hear you with.
Grandma, what big hands you've got.
  –All the better to hold you with.
Grandma, what big teeth you've got.
  –All the better to eat you with.
HELP!

## Unit 8

(Class Cassette: Parts 1 and 2 = Home Cassette: Parts B and C)

*Unit 8, Part 1. Listen and count in tens.*
1. Count to 50, in tens.
2. Count from 20 to 70, in tens.
3. Count from 40 to 100, in tens.
4. Count from 30 to 90, in tens.

*Unit 8, Part 2. Listen and do the actions.*
You're going to hop. Ready? 1 . . . 2 . . . 3 . . . hop. Now, pick up a tape measure. Measure the distance. How far did you hop?

*Unit 8, Part 3. Listen and give your friend the right pictures.*
1. Can I have the ruler, please?
2. Can I have the eraser, please?
3. Can I have the pencil, please?
4. Can I have the tape measure, please?
5. Can I have the scissors, please?
6. Can I have the glue, please?
7. Can I have the scales, please?
8. Can I have the felt tip, please?

*Unit 8, Part 4. Listen. Tell your family where to stand. Then take their photo.*
Mum, dad, grandma and grandad, stand over there. Pete, stand in front of mum. Julie, stand in front of grandad. Grandad, stand next to mum. Now smile. Say cheese. Thank you.

## Unit 9

(Class Cassette: Parts 2, 3 and 1 = Home Cassette: Parts A, B and C (+D))

*Unit 9, Part 1. Listen and do the actions.*
Ready? Hold an ice-cream in your right hand. Open your mouth. Lick the ice-cream. Swallow. Lick your lips. Yum.

*Unit 9, Part 2. Listen and give true answers.*
1. What's your favourite food?
2. What's your favourite drink?
3. What's your favourite ice-cream?
4. What's your favourite toy?

*Unit 9, Part 3. Listen and give true answers.*
1. Do you like chocolate ice-cream?
2. Do you like chocolate cake?
3. Do you like coke?
4. Do you like ketchup?

*Unit 9, Part 4. Listen and join in.*
I like coffee. I like tea.    I like Annie in with me.
I like coffee. I like tea.    I like Andy in with me.
I like coffee. I like tea.    I like Charlie in with me.

## Unit 10

(Class Cassette: Parts 1 and 2 = Home Cassette: Parts A and B)

*Unit 10, Part 1. Listen, look at each picture. Say yes or no.*
Picture 1. Does he have a round shaped face?
Picture 2. Does he have a square shaped nose?
Picture 3. Does he have two triangle shaped eyes?
Picture 4. Does she have a heart shaped mouth?
Picture 5. Does she have a rectangle shaped face?
Picture 6. Does she have two square shaped ears?

*Unit 10, Part 2. Listen and draw the right shape with your finger.*
1. Draw a big round shaped face.
2. Draw two small round shaped eyes.
3. Draw two small triangle shaped eyebrows.
4. Draw a big egg shaped nose.
5. Draw a small heart shaped mouth.
6. Draw two small square shaped ears.

## Unit 11

(Class Cassette: Parts 1, 2 and 3 = Home Cassette: Parts A, B and C)

*Unit 11, Part 1. Listen and ask your friend for the right pictures.*
1. Can I have some chocolate and some ice-cream and some coke please?
2. Can I have some cookies and some crisps and some milk please?

*Unit 11, Part 2. Listen and say what you want.*
1. Do you want some lemonade or orange juice?
2. Do you want a sandwich or a cookie?
3. Do you want a coke or a glass of water?

*Unit 11, Part 3. Listen and say yes or no.*
1. Do you like milk?
2. Do you like chocolate?
3. Do you like swimming?
4. Do you like skipping?

*Unit 11, Part 4. Listen and write in the correct numbers on the pictures.*
Water is number 16. 16.
Computer games is number 60. 60.
Yellow is number 40. 40.
Grey is number 14. 14.
Purple is number 18. 18.
Black is number 30. 30.
White is number 90. 90.
Orange is number 19. 19.

*Unit 11, Part 5. Listen and join in.*
I'm a little teapot, short and stout.
Here's my handle. Here's my spout.
This is my saucer. This is my cup.
Pour in the milk and drink it up.

## Unit 12

(Class Cassette: Parts 4 and 1 = Home Cassette: Parts A and D)

*Unit 12, Part 1.  You're going to play with a balloon. Listen and do the actions.*
You're holding a big round red balloon. Hold it in both hands. Throw it high into the air. Watch it fall. Catch it. Put it down.

*Unit 12, Part 2.  Listen and hold up the right pieces.*
Ring . . . a ring . . . of roses.
A pocket full . . . of posies.
A-tishoo . . . A-tishoo.
We all . . . fall . . . down.

*Unit 12, Part 3.  Listen again. Learn the rhyme. Play the game.*
Ring a ring·of roses. A pocket full of posies. A-tishoo, A-tishoo. We all fall down.

*Unit 12, Part 4.  Listen. Draw the shape of the balloons with your finger.*
1. A big round red balloon.
2. A small heart shaped green balloon.
3. A long thin yellow balloon.
4. A long twisty purple balloon.